THE KEW GARDENER'S GUIDE TO

GROWING VEGETABLES

THE KEW GARDENER'S GUIDE TO

GROWING
VEGETABLES

THE ART AND SCIENCE TO
GROW YOUR OWN VEGETABLES

HÉLÈNA DOVE

FRANCES
LINCOLN

Contents

6   **INTRODUCTION TO GROWING VEGETABLES**

—

28   **PLANTS**

—

30   Okra
31   Leek
32   Onion

—

34   **PROJECT 1: RAISED BEDS**

—

36   Shallot
37   Spring onion
38   Garlic
40   American groundnut
41   Celery
42   Celeriac
43   Peanut
44   Asparagus

—

46   **PROJECT 2: CREATING AN ASPARAGUS BED**

—

48   Beetroot
49   Chard
50   Swede
51   Kale
53   Calabrese

—

54   **PROJECT 3: USING VEGETABLES AS A DECORATIVE DISPLAY**

—

56   Cauliflower
57   Cabbage
59   Brussels sprout
60   Kohl rabi
61   Sprouting broccoli
62   Turnip
63   Pak choi
64   Mizuna
65   Komatsuna
66   Pepper
67   Endive
68   Chicory
69   Miner's lettuce
70   Seakale
71   Cucumber

—

72   **PROJECT 4: CREATING A WILDLIFE-FRIENDLY VEGETABLE GARDEN**

—

74   Courgette and summer squash
75   Winter squash
76   Pumpkin
77   Globe artichoke
78   Carrot

80 PROJECT 5: BUILDING A ROOT CLAMP

82 Rocket
83 Florence fennel
84 Soya bean
86 Jerusalem artichoke
87 Sweet potato

88 PROJECT 6: SWEET-POTATO SLIPS

90 Lettuce
92 Cucamelon
93 Watercress

94 PROJECT 7: ROOTING WATERCRESS

96 Oca
97 Parsnip
98 Parsley root
99 Runner bean
100 French bean
101 Tomatillo
102 Pea

104 PROJECT 8: WINDOWSILL SALADS

106 Mangetout and sugarsnap pea
107 Radish
108 Radish pod
109 Rhubarb

110 PROJECT 9: FORCED RHUBARB

112 Buckler-leaf sorrel
113 Agretti
114 Yacon
115 Tomato

118 PROJECT 10: SEED SAVING

120 Aubergine
121 Potato

124 PROJECT 11: FESTIVE WINTER VEGETABLES

126 Spinach
127 Lamb's lettuce

128 PROJECT 12: NATURAL SUPPORTS FOR BROAD BEANS

130 Broad bean
131 Sweetcorn

132 Troubleshooting
136 What to do when
142 Index
144 Acknowledgments

Introduction to growing vegetables

—

THE VALUE OF VEGETABLES

For many people, growing food is more than just a pastime – it is an obsession and a way of life. As well as an engaging hobby, growing the ingredients for your kitchen has many other benefits, too.

When raising food from seed or a young plant, choice can be made over cultivation techniques, and for many gardeners this will include not using chemicals and instead raising vegetables organically. Chemicals are commonly used in commercial food growing to deal with pests and diseases, and to produce the most perfect harvest possible. These chemicals effect the environment around us, and residues inevitably end up on the plate. The home grower can use techniques that do not include chemicals to combat pests and diseases (see Troubleshooting, pages 132–5).

By walking into the back garden or cycling to the allotment you can also benefit the environment by reducing the air miles that so much other food travels. Much of the food in supermarkets is flown in from around the world or is transported in trucks from different parts of the country.

The use of fuel and packaging is detrimental to the environment, and to the food itself. Once vegetables are harvested, they start to lose nutrients, sweetness and taste – all culminating in the view that locally grown, fresh harvests are best.

Certain crops do not easily survive transportation, even if from a local producer. Crops such as chard tend to wilt and, although completely edible, do not look appetizing by the time they end up in the shops. Other crops are often not available as they do not sell to a wide range of people or may not look perfect to the consumer. Heritage vegetables often fall into this category because they may look slightly unusual: for example, the cracked-skinned beetroot 'Rouge Crapaudine' (nicknamed toad beetroot). They may also be non-uniform, often expensive to crop (as they are not high-yielding) or suffer from diseases. However, heritage crops often provide different tastes or textures: for example, the heritage tomato 'Ananas', introduced in 1894, has a delicious pineapple flavour.

OPPOSITE Taking a summer harvest including radish, peppers, courgettes and lettuce directly from plot to plate is a pure delight.

As well as heritage crops, growing your own vegetables means you can try out crops that have previously been unsuited to your local climate, making these vegetables either non-existent or very scarce to buy. Oca (*Oxalis tuberosa*) is an Andean crop with a delicious lemony root and is currently being bred to produce marketable harvests, but one plant at home gives enough to try out this interesting ingredient.

Freshly harvested vegetables also encourage more home-cooked dishes and inevitably a good diet with plenty of fresh produce, while the physical action of creating and tending a vegetable garden gives gentle and fulfilling exercise. Gardening has been proven to help lift mood and there is a considerable satisfaction in being outdoors, reaping the rewards of what was sown.

WHAT WE CAN GROW AND WHERE

Understanding your growing space is key to a successful vegetable garden, and getting the most from the plot. Before even putting a seed into the ground, observe the space: where does the sun fall and at what time of day; what type of soil do you have; what is growing well already? The answers to these questions will indicate what crops will thrive.

Hardiness

Researching the hardiness zone your vegetable garden lies in will give an indication of which plants will grow well there. All plants are given a hardiness rating by a governing body such as the Royal Horticultural Society (RHS) in the UK. As a rough guide, plants with a rating of H1–2 are frost tender and will not survive freezing conditions: H3 plants are half hardy and tolerate some cold; H4–7 plants will live through cold spells, with H4 plants surviving −10°C/14°F to −5°C/23°F, and H7 plants living through temperatures colder than −20°C/−4°F.

One way to grow plants that may not thrive in cold conditions is to provide a protected growing area such as a greenhouse or a cloched area. Being able to provide artificial heat to the protected cropping space will again extend the range of vegetables that can be grown, as well as prolong the season of harvest.

When growing vegetables, it is worth noting that some do not like extremely hot temperatures: for example, plants in the brassica family prefer temperatures a little cooler than crops such as tomatoes, so either grow these cooler crops in spring and autumn or provide light shade where possible. Alternatively, use bolt-resistant cultivars such as pak choi 'Glacier', which withstand high temperatures.

Microclimates

Each growing area will have its own microclimate, which is affected by the lay of the land and hard landscaping. It will influence where crops are planted and what will thrive overall. Researching the equivalent sea level of the garden will give a general feeling for what plants will thrive in the growing area. The higher above sea level the plot is, the cooler and more exposed it is likely to be. Exposed sites will suffer from the wind, which can be

Once the forced rhubarb is harvested, allow the remaining stems to grow in the light.

Forcing

One way of extending a season of harvest is by forcing vegetables such as rhubarb, seakale and chicory. This process works by covering the crop in complete darkness and providing some extra heat, either by bringing them indoors or by surrounding them with a warming material such as bubble wrap, horticultural fleece or manure. Providing these conditions forces the plant to use energy reserves to grow and search for the light, which gives faster growth and leads to a sweeter crop. These crops are often available several weeks earlier than their non-forced counterparts. See also Forced rhubarb, page 110.

detrimental to crops, cause leaf damage and make it difficult for pollinators to fly from plant to plant to pollinate them. The topography of the plot should be noted; if it is on a slope, the aspect of the garden will be accentuated, and the drainage will need improving at the top and possibly also at the bottom.

In more exposed sites you will be able to grow coastal plants well, such as seakale and cabbage, but you may want to create shelters using hedges or hard landscaping to provide sheltered spots for more tender plants such as tomatoes.

The aspect of the garden relates to where the sun falls. In the northern hemisphere, if the garden faces south, it will be warm and have light for much of the day. North-facing gardens are shadier and cooler, suiting leafy crops.

Look around the garden for frost pockets and sheltered spots. Frost pockets are most easily noted in the cold months and are likely to occur in small dips in the land where cold air can collect. Such pockets remain cold longer into spring and get cooler early at the end of the season, meaning it is best to avoid planting tender plants such as tomatoes and peppers in these areas. Sheltered spots are those that are not open to heavy winds and tend to be a little protected, often giving them a microclimate, which is a little warmer. Sheltered spots are fantastic for planting not only tender vegetables such as tomatoes and peppers, but also perennial plants including globe artichokes which will appreciate the early warmth sheltered spots receive.

Testing home soil
Soil pH can be tested at home with a pH kit or probe. To test its texture, squeeze a ball of moist soil. If it feels gritty and falls to pieces, it has a high sand content, and if the ball feels smooth and moulds to a ball it is clay soil.

A home soil-testing kit does not need to be expensive to buy, and the results can be invaluable.

Soil
The soil is an essential part of the vegetable garden and understanding its qualities will aid your decisions about how to cultivate the site and what crops will thrive.

Soil is made up of three main particles – clay, silt and sand – which give the ground its primary properties. Clay has the smallest particles and it binds well to other particles, giving a fertile soil that retains water well. It takes longer to warm in spring and can drain very slowly, resulting in a wet soil that is easily compacted. Sand particles are the largest, providing a free-draining soil that warms quickly in spring but is not particularly fertile and can dry out quickly. Silt is the third particle type; it is of a medium size and has properties somewhere between clay and soil. It is very unlikely that your garden has soil that is solely clay, silt or sand. Instead, it is probably a mix of the three. A loam soil is considered to be the perfect combination of the three, with 40 per cent sand, 40 per cent silt and 20 per cent clay.

To test what type of soil is within your plot, you can send a sample to a professional lab, which can also report on fertility and pH. Alternatively, a rough soil test can be undertaken at home (see box, above). Once the soil type is understood, there are several ways to potentially improve it through cultivation. The addition of well-rottted organic matter such as manure can improve drainage in clay soils, and it adds fertility and moisture retention to sandy soils. Add as much organic matter as possible to areas where there may be low fertility, poor drainage or poor moisture retention. It is hard to completely change the soil type in the long term, so it is best to grow what will thrive in the existing plot. Root crops like free-draining, sandy soil, whereas brassicas grow well in fertile, heavy soil.

The other aspect of the soil that will affect what crops thrive is its pH, which measures how acidic or alkaline the soil is on a scale of 0–14. A pH of 7 is considered as neutral, 14 is extremely alkali and 0 is extremely acidic. Most soils are slightly acidic – a healthy soil usually falls in a pH range of 5.5–7.5. There is very little that can be done to change a soil pH, so it is best to match the crop to the soil.

In certain situations, acid-loving crops can be grown in ericaceous (acidic) soil in pots: for example, potatoes appreciate slight acidity, and this also helps to deter scab developing on their skins. Lime can be applied to raise soil pH or sulphur applied to lower it, but this slight change to pH will be only temporary.

Light
The last aspect to consider in the growing space is where the light lands. Walls, hedges, fences and trees will cast shade, either permanently or for part of the day. This shade can be used to grow vegetables that like cooler conditions in midsummer, or to hold back plug plants that are growing too quickly. Working out which part of the plot gets the most sun will indicate where heat-loving crops need to be placed. When erecting tall items such as bean supports or sheds, be aware of what shade these will cast and when (see also Natural supports for broad beans, page 128).

RIGHT PLANT, RIGHT PLACE
Understanding the vegetable plot is extremely important. However, rather than spending time trying to change what nature has provided, success is more likely to be found in choosing the right vegetables for the right places.

When planning a traditional vegetable garden, similar crops are grouped together, and their growing space rotated annually. This practice helps to reduce the build-up of certain soil-borne diseases that some groups carry. It also looks at the different nutrients that the groups of crops need so as not to deplete the soil, and it ensures the correct conditions are created for that group. There are many ways of classifying the crops – the following is simply one of them.

Alliums
Alliums are a staple of the vegetable garden encompassing crops such as onions (*A. cepa*), garlic (*A. sativum*) and leeks (*A. ampeloprasum*). Because of its distinctive taste, most recipes include a member of the *Allium* genus, which makes it a useful crop to grow in the vegetable garden. As many alliums can be dried and stored, the home grower can utilize their allium crop year-round.

The strong onion smell that allium crops exude can also be useful to disguise the smell of other crops in a form of pest control: for example, growing alliums around carrots can deter carrot fly (see Troubleshooting, page 134) as the alliums mask the smell of the carrots when the leaves are damaged by thinning or weeding.

Alliums do suffer from a pest called allium leaf miner, which lays its eggs in the base of the allium leaf in spring and autumn. The hatching larvae eat the stems and leaves of the plant, causing distorted growth. This can be stopped by protecting with micromesh.

Alliums are monocots, producing single strap-like leaves, usually above a bulbous base. Most parts of the plants are edible to some extent – from the onion bulb, the leek stem and the garlic flowers.

Most alliums are annuals while some are perennials such as Babington leeks (*A. ampeloprasum* var. *babingtonii*) or evergreens such as Welsh onions (*A. fistulosum*). Many alliums come from hot dry climates so want free-draining soil that gets baked in the hot months. They will often survive cold weather, but do not thrive in very wet conditions.

Brassicas

Members of the brassica family (Brassicaceae) all carry some of the mustard flavour that is created by these plants as a defence against pests. There is a large range of adaptations within this family, giving leaf crops such as rocket (*Eruca vesicaria*), edible inflorescences such as cauliflower (*Brassica oleracea* Botrytis Group) and stem crops such as turnips (*B. rapa*).

Brassica plants enjoy cooler conditions than some crops and often take a long time in the ground to mature. They are some of the hardiest plants in the vegetable garden, providing a lot of the fresh harvests in winter. Interestingly, some of the staple brassica crops are all adaptations of the same wild cabbage, *B. oleracea*. Cabbages (*B. oleracea* Capitata Group) are the large terminal bud, sprouts (Gemmifera Group) are the compact axillary buds and cauliflowers (Botrytis

Group) are the edible inflorescences of the plant.

Brassicas prefer acidic soil but tolerate more alkaline conditions, which is particularly useful if the growing area suffers from the disease clubroot (see page 135) because raising pH will deter this condition. They are also vulnerable to several pests including pigeons, cabbage white butterflies and root fly (see Troubleshooting, pages 132–4), all of which can be deterred with barrier methods of pest control. Brassica roots can easily be damaged if the plants experience high winds; to ensure the roots are secure, always heel in well and sink the plants low into the ground when transplanting to give stability.

Fruiting vegetables

When cultivating fruiting crops, the part that is primarily being eaten is the fleshy seed container, although other bits of the plant are also edible, such as the seeds in some *Cucurbita pepo* (squash and pumpkins). Technically fruits and not vegetables, there is often summer sweetness to these crops, and they add colour to the vegetable garden with hot colours including reds, oranges and purples (see Using vegetables as a decorative display, page 54). Some of the most commonly grown fruiting crops include tomatoes (*Solanum lycopersicum*), peppers (*Capsicum annuum*) and aubergines (*Solanum melongena*).

Mainly frost tender, fruiting crops often require heat to germinate and a long growing season so need to be started off indoors and transplanted

One way of classifying crops is into (clockwise from top left) alliums, brassicas, fruiting vegetables, roots, legumes and salads.

once there is little risk of frost. These crops need a hot spot or greenhouse to thrive and will generally benefit from well-mulched ground, which will add fertility, retain moisture and suppress weed growth.

Salad crops

This is a large grouping of plants from many different families, many of which develop edible leaves that make fine additions to salads and cooked dishes. These range from crunchy heads of lettuce (*Lactuca sativa*) to rich spinach (*Spinacia oleracea*) and overwintered chicons of bitter chicory (*Cichorium intybus*). Leafy crops are often easily grown in containers, with cut-and-come-again plants giving several crops from one plant.

Leafy crops can have quite small seeds, which can be tricky to germinate *in situ* as they struggle in soil that does not have a very fine tilth. For this reason, they are often more successful when started off in modules and subsequently transplanted. They can be sensitive to temperature, and will not germinate when it is too cool, but will run to seed when it becomes too hot,

It is always a pleasure to harvest a head of lettuce for a summer salad.

especially brassica leaves such as rocket (*Eruca vesicaria*) and lettuce. Once leafy crops bolt, in order to produce flower heads, the leaves very often become inedible: for example, lettuce turns bitter and mustardy-flavoured leaves become much hotter in taste. Leafy crops benefit from some shade in the hotter months, so can be grown in a corner of the vegetable garden that does not get full sun or as an intercrop with bigger plants, which cast shade (see Succession/Intercropping/Catch cropping, page 24).

Legumes

The legume family consists of many staple plants found within the vegetable garden, including peas (*Pisum sativum*) and beans. These are quite often climbing plants, and all have the ability to fix nitrogen through symbiotic relationships with bacteria in nodules on their roots. This ability means that they need less artificial feeding and that

they leave a fertile soil behind after the crop is harvested.

The most common focus in the legume family is its edible immature seeds, as in peas, but often the seed pod is also delicious as with French beans (*Phaseolus vulgaris*). The young growing tips and tendrils such as pea shoots are often a delicacy and an interesting addition to salads. The seeds of legumes are fairly easy to save (see Seed saving, page 118) and can be dried and stored for winter consumption as is the case for 'Borlotti' French beans.

Roots

Root crops fall roughly into two categories: those growing completely underground; and those that have a good proportion of the edible plant underground, but some showing above. Those developing completely underground such as carrots (*Daucus carota* subsp. *sativus*) and parsnips (*Pastinaca sativa*) are true root crops, while tuberous crops such as potatoes (*Solanum tuberosum*) are stem adaptations. Those with visible growth on top of the soil such as beetroot (*Beta vulgaris*) are swollen stem bases, and the roots will be visible below the storage organ when harvested. In all instances, the plant has chosen to adapt and swell part of its anatomy to become a storage organ, which humans have learnt to cultivate and enjoy over the centuries.

Most root crops enjoy free-draining soil as they often rot if growing in too much water. A sandy, stone-free and friable soil will also give less resistance to a developing root; if the delicate root tip hits an obstacle it can break and the root will start to develop from further up, creating a forked or stunted vegetable, which is an issue for carrots and parsnips grown for sale and the display bench.

PERENNIALS, ANNUALS AND BIENNIALS

The life cycles of the crops will guide their placement within the vegetable garden. Perennial plants live for three or more years and, therefore, need to have a permanent position. Perennial plants are not harvested in their first year, while they establish, but after that will give a delicious crop early in spring when little else is growing.

Most other vegetables are treated as annual crops, which complete their life cycle within a year. These are often started from seed and include crops such as lettuce and courgettes. Some crops are perennial in their natural environment but will not thrive through a cold wet winter: for example, some

peppers (which can be overwintered in a greenhouse) and runner beans.

The third life cycle encountered in the vegetable garden is of biennial plants such as carrots and parsnips. These produce their seed in the second year of growth, which is useful to know if planning to save seed (see Seed saving, page 118). In terms of harvesting, they are treated as annuals, being harvested within the year of planting.

PREPARING THE PLOT

Once the decision has been made as to what is to be grown, it is essential to get the growing space ready, starting with the most important aspect – the soil.

The first task is removing any weeds, because most crops dislike competition and it can be hard to tell which young plant your crop is and which is a weed, plus some weeds carry diseases, which can spread to crops. Observe and see what weeds are growing; are they annual ones such as hairy bittercress (*Cardamine hirsuta*) or perennials such as hedge bindweed (*Calystegia sepium*)? Annual weeds can be hoed off and, although they might reappear from the seeds stored in the ground, are easily managed with continuous hoeing while small; aim not to let them seed. Perennial weeds can be dug out or managed in the no-dig method of cultivation, where they are weakened by continuous hoeing and removal of the green growth and smothered with mulch, which over the course of several years will kill the underground roots. Be aware if digging perennial weeds that many of them will reproduce easily from tiny amounts of root and stem left

Mulching soil in autumn or spring helps to suppress weeds.

in the ground, often meaning that if they are not fully removed they will regrow – this may be clever for the plant but is extremely frustrating for the gardener. All vegetable gardens have weeds but staying on top of them, and learning which ones are edible, will mean they are only a tiny part of the growing experience.

The next step is cultivating and feeding the soil, with the aim of creating a friable soil with no large lumps so that the vegetables can easily send their roots down to search for food and water. One of the easiest ways to achieve this is through no-dig cultivation. The method involves applying around 5cm/2in of mulch to the plot in autumn or early spring and spreading it evenly. This then forms the top layer of the beds, which can be planted and sown into directly. This method copies soil formation in nature, where organic matter falls on to the top of the soil and slowly breaks down, being moved around by worms and other soil-dwellers. This mulch layer will suppress most annual weed growth and, because the seedbed is not being dug over, no stored seeds are being brought to the surface to germinate. It also weakens and kills perennial weeds over time (roughly three years). Plots cultivated with no-dig are fertile, and the fertility is where most of the vegetable roots reside, in the topsoil. Also, the mulch layer helps to lock in moisture, which is an advantage of mulching in the wetter seasons. The mulch can be well-rotted compost, manure or a mixture of these. As well as buying in compost, the vegetable gardener is likely to have a compost heap where they put kitchen waste, annual weeds, some grass clippings and chipped woody material.

Another way to add fertility to soil, suppress weeds and retain moisture is to grow a green manure such as *Phacelia tanacetifolia* or *Sinapis alba*. With this method, large amounts of seed of these plants are scattered on to the earth and allowed to grow into a thick green canopy, eventually either being dug into the earth, or hoed off, leaving the roots in the ground and the green foliage sent to the compost heap to eventually return as mulch. Green manures are fantastic if ground will be bare for a period of time, such as the space where tender plants will eventually be grown.

Essential kit
To undertake a year tending a vegetable garden, here is some essential kit:
- Dutch hoe – for quickly weeding through the beds
- border fork – for lifting root crops
- rake – for creating an even surface to plant into
- hand trowel – for planting out vegetables
- secateurs – for harvesting fruiting crops such as tomatoes
- watering can – for watering and feeding crops
- compost – for sowing seeds into
- modular trays and pots – for starting off plants
- twine – for tying in plants such as beans, cucumbers and tomatoes
- canes and supports – for climbing plants.

Equipment should be cleaned after every use to stop diseases spreading around the vegetable plot, and this practice also keeps all tools in good order. Wash pots with soapy water and wipe down tool blades with an oily rag. Annual maintenance on tools includes oiling wooden elements and sharpening metal edges on hoes and spades.

Useful extras
As well as the essential tools, there are a few additions that will increase the productivity of the vegetable garden:
- heated propagator – for extending the sowing season at the beginning of the year
- thermometer – for ensuring plants are raised at the correct temperature
- horticultural fleece and cloches – to protect plants in the cold months
- cold frame – to aid hardening off of young plants.

CHOOSING AND BUYING
Because the vegetable garden is a mainly annual affair, the whole plot is replanted every year, which gives opportunities to try new crops, new cultivars and to learn from any mistakes of the previous year. Planning for the forthcoming season often takes place in the depths of winter, while curled up with a seed catalogue.

One of the first decisions to make is what crops to grow. Consider which vegetables will thrive in the growing space. There is little point in trying to grow heat-loving crops such as tomatoes in an outdoor space that does not get full sun; however, this crop could be grown in a pot, which could be moved to a protected area outdoors in summer.

Another aspect to settle is which harvests will be enjoyed by the recipients – growing an entire bed of turnips just to discover there is no one in the family who likes them can be very disheartening.

A further consideration is the financial value of the crop, especially if growing space is limited. Vegetables such as cabbages are cheap to buy in shops and take up a fair amount of room in the plot, whereas asparagus is a delicacy and expensive to purchase.

Another decision to make is whether to start the crops from seed or plug plants. There are many companies now offering plug plants, which will be sent out throughout the year; although these are slightly more expensive than a packet of seed, there is no need for a propagation area, and their use is time-saving, which can suit some people. There will often be slightly less cultivar choice for plug plants, but there is less concern over germination success of seeds, which can occasionally mean an entire crop failure. Some vegetables are easier to purchase as plants or crowns than to start from seed, especially perennial plants such as rhubarb and asparagus, where buying a crown in autumn will give a harvest at least a year earlier than when starting from seed.

However, starting vegetables from seed has many advantages. Seed is relatively cheap, and one packet can often last for many years, depending on seed viability, or can be portioned out and swapped with fellow growers. The range of cultivars when growing from seed is extremely wide, and here again the grower can make informed choices, looking for cultivars that match their requirements. Compact cultivars are ideal for small plots of land or growing in pots: for example, tumbling tomatoes easily grow in a hanging basket and take up a lot less space than a large bush tomato. More recent cultivars have often been bred to show some pest and disease resistance, so for plots

where carrot fly is an issue the carrot cultivar 'Resistafly' has been bred for a higher tolerance. Other advantages may include choosing organic seed for a chemical-free plot, F1 cultivars for the beginner who wants a reliable harvest or heritage varieties for those wanting to explore this area of vegetable growing. There is also the option to save seed from crops to grow the next year (see Seed saving, page 118). This is a rewarding process and the grower can develop strains that crop particularly well in their vegetable garden, as well as being cheaper than buying. If saving seed, research to see what crops will come true, and avoid saving seed from crops that have experienced disease. One of the advantages of seed from merchants is that they have generally been tested for germination rates, do not carry disease and will come true.

SOWING

Most vegetables start life as a seed, which needs to be germinated, grown on and ends up as a delicious harvest. In many cases, the seeds can be sown directly into the ground where they are to remain. Before sowing seeds *in situ*, check with a soil thermometer that the soil temperature is high enough for germination to occur, otherwise the seed is likely to rot off and need to be resown. Most seeds need a minimum of 7°C/45°F, but for more tender vegetables the optimum temperature can range from 15°C/59°F to 21°C/70°F. Although soil can be pre-warmed with horticultural fleece or cloches, it is usually better to wait until the ambient temperature warms the soil naturally.

Crop rotation

Crop rotation is the process of moving the crop groups around the plot to avoid the build-up of diseases and pests, and the depletion of certain nutrients from the soil. Using the no-dig method of cultivation does reduce these issues because the top layer of ground in which the plants grow is renewed every year (see Preparing the plot, page 17).

Growers can rotate their crops as they like, whether it is within a season or annually, but below is a basic four-year rotation plan. Fruiting crops and leaves are not part of the rotation plan as they do not suffer too highly from soil diseases. Brassicas need a lot of nitrogen, so follow well behind legumes, which fix nitrogen thereby increasing the available amounts in the ground, whereas root crops do not require a lot of this element so will happily follow behind brassicas. For a three-year rotation cycle, roots and alliums can easily be moved around together.

A four-year rotation plan for a vegetable garden, such as this one, helps minimize the build up of pests and diseases.

Once spring sunshine has done its job, direct sowing can begin in earnest.

The general rule of thumb is to sow seeds twice the depth that they are tall. Station sow large seeds such as broad beans; that is, sow each seed at the final spacing distance. To ensure a full row, two seeds can be sown per planting hole and then one seedling be discarded once germination occurs. For smaller seeds such as carrots, which want to be shallow in the ground, hoe a shallow drill and broadcast sow thickly along this line, not worrying about distances between the seed. Backfill this drill, watering well. Once germination occurs, thin out the plants until they are evenly spaced at the final distances.

Seeds that require high temperatures to germinate (usually around 21°C/70°F), a long growing season and are frost tender, such as tomatoes and peppers, need to be germinated in a protected environment where ideal conditions can be given. Check the requirements of the individual crop (see plant profiles, pages 28–131), but generally start in a seed tray filled with seed compost, thinly sow the seed (to avoid competition and leggy growth once germination occurs), cover with compost or vermiculite, and water from the bottom by placing the seed tray in a drip tray. The vermiculite helps to retain moisture on the top of the seed tray and thus aids better germination. Using a clear-lidded propagator also helps to retain heat and moisture, but be careful to allow good airflow to avoid damping off (see Troubleshooting, page 135), and clean the propagator in soapy water between uses.

Some seeds including lettuce need a little light for germination and, in these instances, sowing on to the top of the compost and giving a light sprinkle of vermiculite is ideal.

Once the seedlings have germinated, prick out into modules or pots, to give the seedlings space to grow their true leaves. When pricking out, use a pencil, label or dibber to scoop out the plant, lightly holding the seed leaves, which will eventually die back; do not touch the roots or stem as this can stunt growth. Ensure these seedlings are firmed in and watered well. Some crops will want potting up further and transplanting into larger pots. Transplanting is the practice of giving a crop more root space to grow into once their roots have filled their current growing space, be it transplanting a pepper plant from a module to a small pot, or transplanting a lettuce from a module to the open ground.

Apart from true roots crops such as parsnips and carrots (see Roots, page 16), most vegetables can be grown in modules and transplanted once large enough. The benefits of this method include a larger weight of harvest from the growing space, as rather than the crops taking up space while germinating and establishing, which can be over a month, the growing space can be filled with a more mature plant. Sowing under glass gives plants a better start in life as there tend to be fewer pests indoors, and those that occur are often more easily observed and managed. Seed tends to go farther when started in modules as it is effectively station sowing for all crops rather than just

Directly sowing seed into a drill is essential for crops such as carrots and parsnips.

the larger seeds. Vegetable plants sown *in situ* are more prone to attack from pests and diseases but are often stronger plants in the long run. They also benefit from rainwater and from food from the soil, which lessens the responsibility of the grower.

Crops.such as cabbages, tomatoes and peppers are better transplanted as large specimens; in this case, pot them up from modules into individual 9cm/3½in pots, or possibly even larger ones. Knock or ease each seedling out of its module, retaining as much soil as possible around the roots. Add a little compost to the bottom of the new pot, place in the seedling and fill in around the side of the seedling up to the existing nursery line, which is the level of the top of the compost the seedling was previously sitting in. Firm the soil with fingers and water well. Gradually

transplant, in stages, into slightly larger containers. Do not repot into a container considerably larger than the current growing pot, as the extra growing medium will simply retain water and may cause the roots to rot.

HARDENING OFF

If plants have been germinated and started life within a sheltered structure such as a windowsill or greenhouse, they need to be hardened off before planted outdoors. This process allows plants to adjust not only to the colder, less humid environment in the garden, but also to the strong winds and heavy rainfall. If a cold frame is available, transfer the plants there; keep the lid off during the day and replace it at night. Within a week, start keeping the lid off overnight unless extreme cold is predicted. After another week, these plants should be ready to plant out into their final positions, although horticultural fleece may be necessary for any forecast temperature drops.

If a cold frame is not available, move the trays outdoors just during the day for a week, and then for another week leave them outdoors overnight in a sheltered spot with fleece laid over. This process is extremely important in spring when soil and atmospheric temperatures are low and more unpredictable.

PLANTING OUT

When planting out, it is important to have the site prepared before the crops need transplanting (see Preparing the plot, page 17). Traditionally, vegetable beds have rows or blocks of crops, making it easier to weed, observe any

Growing crops in rows allows for optimum spacings.

SUCCESSION/INTERCROPPING/ CATCH CROPPING

When a beginner to vegetable gardening, it is all too easy to plant out blocks of plants at a time, which often leads to a glut of crops all being ready at once. Once the grower is confident, using succession planting will help to avoid gluts. Crops such as radish, beetroot and lettuce can easily be grown in succession, sowing a small amount every week or two. Some crops can be sown closer together and the thinnings harvested.

Another way to extend the season of a crop is to grow different cultivars: for example, early and main-crop peas take different times to mature, and if sown at the same time can give a harvest of peas over four weeks rather than two.

It is also important to use as much of the ground in the vegetable plot as possible. This not only provides the potential for a fantastic harvest, but also reduces space for weeds to grow. Intercropping and catch cropping are two methods of utilizing space. Intercropping is where two crops can grow alongside each other until maturity: for example, growing trailing plants such as cucumbers or squash around the base of tall or climbing plants including beans and sweetcorn. Catch cropping involves quick-maturing vegetables grown in between slower-growing plants: for example, radishes grown in between parsnip seed, which also helps to mark out the row, or beetroot between Brussels sprouts. Intercropping and catch cropping are particularly useful in raised beds (see page 34).

issues and access plants for harvesting. To create even rows, run lines and use a ruler or tape measure to obtain the correct spacings. Dig the correct-sized hole for each plug plant before removing it from its pot, to avoid its roots drying out from too long in the wind or sun. If the roots have begun to grow around the edges of the pot, known as being pot-bound, tickle them loose so they do not grow in on themselves. Transplant into the hole and backfill with soil, ensuring the soil level is the same as the nursery line (unless purposely sinking lower, as with some brassicas, where the new soil level should be above the nursery line as this helps to give secure roots and more support against wind). Firm the soil with fingers, or boot heel for large plants, and water well to ensure soil is in contact with the roots. If crops need supports (see Natural supports for broad beans, page 128), it is best to add these before the crop is planted, or as the plug plant is put in the ground, to avoid damage to established roots.

Companion planting

Flowers can be grown in the vegetable garden and have many benefits for the ecosystem. Companion planting with flowers attracts beneficial insects, which eat pests: for example, pot marigolds (*Calendula officinalis*) attract hoverflies whose young eat aphids, and nasturtiums (*Tropaeolum majus*) are a sacrificial plant for cabbage white caterpillars, attracting them away from the crop plants (see also Troubleshooting, pages 132–4). Both pot marigold and nasturtium flowers are edible and add a splash of colour to summer salads.

Planting French marigolds (*Tagetes*) near tomatoes attracts beneficial pollinators.

PROTECTING VEGETABLES

Vegetables often need a little help from the grower to thrive. This could be shelter from the elements in the form of a greenhouse, protection from pests or supports to climb up (see Natural supports for broad beans, page 128). For those fortunate enough to have access to a greenhouse or an indoor growing space, the range of crops can be much larger and the growing season extended. By growing under glass, seeds can be started earlier, by often as much as a month, and where heat and artificial light can be provided there can be year-round cropping. Ensure the windows in the greenhouse are as clean as possible to allow the maximum amount of light in. If light is an issue, artificial grow lights can be introduced.

If planning to grow vegetables in a greenhouse throughout summer, some shading may be necessary to prevent leaf scorch and to cool the interior when needed, but plants such as tomatoes, peppers and melons will thrive in these conditions, giving harvests earlier in the season, and will continue cropping when outdoor plants have succumbed to frosts. An unheated greenhouse gives the chance to overwinter tender crops such as chilli peppers and cucamelons, which might otherwise be treated as annuals.

Polytunnels are large, plastic-covered structures, which are often placed directly on to open ground and are fantastic for extending the season, with salad crops overwintering well in such a cool but frost-free environment. Another form of covered cropping is a cold frame. These are traditionally used to harden off plants started in a greenhouse that need to be slowly acclimatized to outdoor conditions. Cold frames are very useful when propagating but can also be filled over winter with vegetables such as salads, thereby extending the season.

Those not fortunate enough to have access to a greenhouse, polytunnel or cold frame can instead use horticultural fleece and cloches to give some protection from frost. These are placed on the open ground where the plants are growing *in situ*. They are a fantastic way to warm the soil at the beginning of the season, and to provide protection to early crops; likewise, at the end of the season as the temperatures begin to drop, these mobile covers can extend the cropping season and aid overwintering.

Crops may require protection from pests, and the most common physical barrier is micromesh with holes of 1.3mm/$^{1}/_{20}$in. This extremely fine netting is used against small pests such as carrot fly (see Root flies, page 134) and allium leaf miner. Netting with holes around 5mm/¼in can be used against larger pests such as pigeons and butterflies, where these are an issue on crops including brassicas and legumes.

Other structures in the vegetable garden which add dramatic height are supports for climbing crops. These come in many forms depending on the crop: for example, peas may be given peasticks (branched hazel sticks), 1.5m/5ft tall, to scramble up, while runner beans might find themselves climbing to the top of 3m/10ft birch

poles. Squash may be allowed to scramble over a metal obelisk, French beans look stunning growing up bamboo tepees and cucumbers are at home on a wooden trellis. Allowing plants to climb upwards gives more ground space to crop in, makes for an easier harvest and stops the fruits from sitting on the ground and potentially rotting. Climbing crops also provide a little shade for other vegetables, which may appreciate it; lettuces will enjoy the shade of French beans, which in turn like to have their roots moist – provided by the leaf cover of the lettuces.

WATERING

Plants require water for healthy growth, but they often dislike being overwatered because sitting in too much moisture can cause problems. Watering when plants are initially transplanted is especially important as this helps to create contact between the soil and roots, anchoring in the crops, so ensure the water percolates down below the roots.

After the crops are established, it is important to keep a steady water content in the soil, so check water levels about 5cm/2in below the soil surface; the top is often much drier due to environmental factors such as wind, while the soil below is often still moist.

Rather than watering every day, give the area a thorough watering once or twice a week, as needed. Do this during cool points in the day, to avoid water loss via evaporation. Direct the water at the bases of the plants, avoiding leaves, to stop the spread of disease, and putting the water where it is needed.

Certain crops prefer drier conditions, and others such as onions and squash want no water towards their harvesting period, because this helps them to store for longer. Other vegetables need water at critical points of growth: for example, legumes require little water until flowering. Knowing what the crops need can help minimize water wastage.

MULCHING

Mulching plants helps to retain water in the soil and suppresses weed growth. Organic mulches include well-rotted garden compost and manure. If mulch is applied once crops are in the ground, do not spread it right up to the stems of the plants, and for larger plants create a circular boundary to water into. Other mulches such as straw and woodchip can be used on large crops and perennial vegetables, but they can be a popular home for pests such as slugs. These materials also make fantastic mulches for paths or can be put in the compost heap if well shredded and after several years of rotting down be laid on the beds.

To prevent wastage, water plants directly at their roots and avoid watering any leaves.

Comfrey as a fertilizer
Liquid feeds can be made with plants such as nettle (*Urtica*) and comfrey (*Symphytum officinale*), where the leaves of these plants are left to rot down and release their liquids. Comfrey leaves can also be dug into the planting holes of hungry feeders such as potatoes, squash and beans, giving extra fertility directly where it is needed.

FEEDING

In general, a healthy soil will be fertile enough to support any crop, but occasionally crops require additional feeding (see also Nutrient deficiency, page 135). Fertilizers contain a mixture of the three main nutrients: nitrogen (for leaves), phosphorus (for roots and shoots) and potassium (for flowers and fruits). Organic fertilizers are derived from natural sources such as animals and plants. They can take longer to feed the plant as their large molecules need to be broken down in the soil. Inorganic fertilizers use mined minerals and are fast-acting and concentrated.

Fertilizers can be applied in a solid or liquid form. Liquid fertilizers are applied while watering and are an efficient way of feeding because they go straight to the roots, where needed. Solid fertilizers such as powders and pellets can be added to the soil as topdressings around the plants or as base dressings in the bottom of planting holes. These take slightly longer to break down and are only worthwhile for crops that will be in the ground for a long season, such as large brassicas and squash.

Plants

—

Okra

Abelmoschus esculentus aka bhindi, lady's finger

Okra is a heat-loving annual and is part of the mallow family. The main harvest is of the immature green seed pods, but its leaves are also edible.

WHERE TO GROW
Okra needs a sunny sheltered site, preferably with free-draining soil, although it tolerates heavier clay.

HOW TO GROW
Sow seeds under glass in spring; they need a minimum of 16°C/61°F to germinate, with optimum growing temperatures of 20–30°C/68–86°F. Allow to grow to 15cm/6in tall before hardening off and planting in their final positions; at the same time, stake plants. Pinch out any strong growing tips, to encourage bushy plants.

GROWING TIP
Soaking seeds in warm water for several hours before sowing will give better germination rates.

NOTABLE CULTIVARS
- 'Burgundy' has red skin.
- 'Clemson's Spineless' is extremely vigorous.

Family	Malvaceae
Height	1m/3ft
Spacing	50cm/20in<>plants; 70cm/27in<>rows
Hardiness	Half-hardy annual
Position	Full sun
Edible parts	Seed pods, leaves
Harvest	Late summer–autumn

OKRA POWER
Okra oil is being investigated as a biodiesel, which may be able to power the cars of the future.

Leek

Allium ampeloprasum

Over winter months, leeks are an invaluable crop, adding a sweetness to many dishes and festive occasions (see Festive winter vegetables, page 124). They are a very attractive vegetable with blue leaves, which would not look out of place in an herbaceous display (see Using vegetables as a decorative display, page 54).

WHERE TO GROW

Grow in a sunny site with free-draining soil because leeks do not want to sit in water. They are heavy feeders so add organic matter to their area in the autumn before planting.

HOW TO GROW

Although traditionally sown into a seedbed in early spring and then moved into their final planting site in late spring, leeks can also be started in modules in late winter. They need a temperature of 7°C/45°F to germinate so may need additional heat. Once pencil-sized, transplant the leeks, trimming roots and leaves to make them easier to move, and water in well.

GROWING TIP

To obtain a longer, prized, blanched, white shank, form a deep drill, then dib planting holes into the bottom of this to insert the leeks in. The drill will naturally backfill with water as the plants grow, slowly blanching the stem.

Family
Amaryllidaceae
Height
40cm/16in
Spacing
10cm/4in◇plants;
30cm/12in◇rows
Hardiness
Hardy
Position
Full sun
Edible parts
Leaves
Harvest
Autumn–early spring

LEEK GARDEN
Leeks have been an important plant in Britain for a long time, and Anglo-Saxons referred to the entire vegetable garden as a Leek Garden.

NOTABLE CULTIVARS
- 'Bleu de Solaise' (aka 'Blue Solaise') is a heritage cultivar with blue leaves, which turn purple in the cold months.
- 'Musselburgh' is a very hardy cultivar, which can withstand temperatures of −5°C/23°F.

Onion

Allium cepa

Onions are the basis of so many dishes and a star vegetable in terms of flavour, packing a sweet fragrant punch (see also Festive winter vegetables, page 124). They are an easy crop to grow with a great range of sizes, colours and flavours.

—

WHERE TO GROW

Needs a sunny spot and free-draining soil, with soil of pH 5.5–6.5. Onions have short roots so the top 5–10cm/2–4in of soil needs to be very fertile to feed them while growing.

HOW TO GROW

Start from sets or seeds. If from seed, sow into a shallow tray in late winter and leave in a heat of around 21°C/70°F for best germination. Prick seedlings out into modules once large enough and slowly harden off for planting out. Onions are slow-growing plants, so be prepared to care for them for two months before they are large enough to transplant. Once ready, place seedlings in the ground ensuring not to sink them too deeply, and add a thin layer of mulch. Sets can also be planted out in spring as for transplanting seedlings. Onions tolerate cold weather with some cultivars being overwintered easily from sets, planted out in autumn and harvestable in early summer.

Keep onions weed-free because they easily become smothered and do not bulb up when shaded. Therefore, ensure there is room to hoe between the plants.

Harvest onions once their leaves start to turn yellow. If possible, lay the harvested onions in a dry sunny spot for several days after harvest, to allow them to air dry thoroughly for the optimum storing conditions.

Family
Amaryllidaceae
Height
60cm/24in
Spacing
10cm/4in◇plants;
30cm/12in◇rows
Hardiness
Hardy
Position
Full sun
Edible parts
Bulbs, leaves
Harvest
Mid–late summer

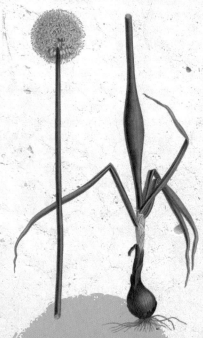

ONION TEARS
When an onion is cut, the cell wall is broken down and it produces a sulphuric acid gas, which causes the human eye to stream. The sulphur compounds within the onion are also what creates its distinctive flavour and give it some antibacterial properties.

GROWING TIP

Onions are prone to bolting if they are planted too early. They may also produce flower spikes towards the end of their maturity; remove these as soon as they are spotted, to stop the plant putting its energy into reproduction.

SETS OR SEED?

Onions can be purchased in two different forms: seeds and sets. Sets are immature onions that have been started from seed late in the previous summer. As they are slightly more advanced at the beginning of the season, they are ideal in areas that have shorter summers or if propagation space is limited.

Starting onions from seeds gives a larger choice of cultivars available to grow, and the gardener gets more plants for less money. Seed can be saved from onions and will come true if no other cultivar is growing nearby (see Seed saving, page 118).

NOTABLE CULTIVARS

- 'Ailsa Craig' is a large, yellow-fleshed heritage onion from 1887.
- 'Red Baron' has red flesh and stores well.
- 'Stuttgarter Giant' is a flattened bulb with yellow flesh.

Raised beds

Raised beds can be extremely useful: their higher growing area can be of fantastic benefit to those who struggle to reach down to the ground. They can also be a way of cultivating in areas with extremely poor or unhealthy soil, by filling them with new organic matter. They are fairly easy to maintain, as the new growing medium should contain very few weeds and can easily have posts erected in the corner, making the addition of netting or fleece incredibly simple.

Such beds can be formed from different materials including timber and brick and can be purchased or assembled with reclaimed materials. When using reclaimed materials, especially timber, it is worth lining the raised bed to protect the growing area from any treatments the timber may previously have undergone so these do not leach into it. When choosing the material, consider how long the raised bed needs to last: bricks are permanent, whereas a small timber frame can easily be moved around. Deciding what height the structure needs to be will affect the material choice: large beds will contain a lot of soil and the sides will need to be able to retain this weight. The bed's width is important because, on average, a person can reach around 60cm/24in comfortably, so there is little point in making the bed more than 1.25m/4ft wide, otherwise it will have to be climbed on to obtain access.

When growing root crops, look at the depth of the bed, too: very high beds are suitable for all crops, but shallow raised beds will not allow for long carrots, so instead sow small types such as 'Paris Market' carrots.

In a raised bed, plant dwarf cultivars or bushy forms of trailing plants. Growing runner beans that reach 3m/10ft high in a bed that is already 1m/3ft high is going to lead to difficult harvesting, whereas dwarf runners reach only 50cm/20in and are perfect for a raised bed. Also use intercropping and catch cropping to make the most of the space (see Succession/ Intercropping/Catch cropping, page 24).

A Low raised beds, 10–30cm/
   4–12in high, can be used to
   convert a weedy area or lawn
   into a bed by filling it with
   compost and keeping it in
   place for one to three years.
B A raised bed can easily be
   divided into sections, and each
   section cultivated differently.
C High raised beds of around
   1m/3ft bring the crops to a
   level accessible for those with
   problems bending down.
D In gardens that suffer from carrot
   fly, carrots and parsnips can be
   grown in a raised bed higher
   than 70cm/28in to avoid damage.
E Urban gardeners can grow
   vegetables in a raised bed, using
   dwarf cultivars to make the most
   of the space.

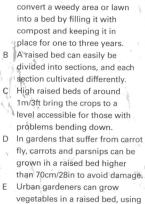

Shallot

Allium cepa

Sweeter and milder in taste than the standard onion, shallots can be used for cooking and pickling or be eaten raw.

WHERE TO GROW

Cultivate in a sunny spot with free-draining soil. Shallots are small plants so can be used to interplant between larger crops.

HOW TO GROW

Start from seeds or sets (see Sets or seed?, page 33). One bulb from a set will produce a clump of shallots, which need to be thinned in spring, whereas seeds produce one shallot per seed. Start seeds under cover in a seed tray or modules, and plant out in late spring, watering in well.

GROWING TIP

Shallots, as for other alliums, do not need watering towards the point of harvesting and will benefit from being laid in a dry sunny spot after harvesting.

Family
Amaryllidaceae
Height
40cm/16in
Spacing
10cm/4in<>plants;
30cm/12in<>rows
Hardiness
Hardy
Position
Full sun
Edible parts
Bulbs, leaves
Harvest
Summer

FROGS AND BANANAS
Some shallots are elongated and slightly curved and have gained the name banana or frog-legs shallots.

NOTABLE CULTIVARS
- 'Jermor', from France, has a slightly pink tinge to its flesh.
- Zebrune' is a banana shallot that reliably produces large bulbs.

Spring onion

Allium cepa aka salad onion, scallions

Spring onions are varieties of *Allium cepa* that do not form a large bulb at the base and are mainly grown for their leaves, which can be eaten raw or cooked.

—

WHERE TO GROW
Needs free-draining, fertile soil with as sunny a spot as can be afforded. As spring onions do not take up much space, they can be used to interplant while larger crops mature.

HOW TO GROW
Start off in modules in late winter through to early summer, sowing several seeds per module, or else sow directly into the soil from early spring where required. When transplanting, set spring onions in a row, or sink the entire module in a cluster. Water in well and harvest what you need as and when. Spring-sown plants will be harvestable after two months, and a continuous supply can be grown if seed is sown every few weeks throughout summer.

GROWING TIP
To harvest in early spring, try sowing a very hardy cultivar in late summer and overwintering it with a little protection.

Family
Amaryllidaceae
Height
40cm/16in
Spacing
2cm/¾in<>plants;
30cm/12in<>rows
Hardiness
Hardy
Position
Full sun
Edible parts
Bulbs, leaves
Harvest
Spring–early summer

WINTER TREAT
Calçots are a type of spring onion celebrated in the Catalonia region of Spain. At the end of January, a festival is held where this vegetable is grilled and consumed in great quantities.

NOTABLE CULTIVARS
- 'North Holland Blood Red' is a red-fleshed spring onion and will develop into a full red onion if left in the ground.
- 'White Lisbon Winter Hardy' is a very hardy cultivar for overwintering and will survive through temperatures of −15°C/5°F.

Garlic

Allium sativum

This is a staple ingredient in many dishes and an easy vegetable to cultivate, making it invaluable in the vegetable garden. It is harvestable in many different stages and can be stored easily, meaning home-grown garlic can be on the menu year-round.

WHERE TO GROW

Needs a sunny spot with free-draining soil to give the best harvest. The site should be weed-free as young garlic will not compete well.

HOW TO GROW

Plant garlic cloves directly in the ground from mid-autumn until mid-winter. Ensure the cloves are just under the surface when planted, because birds often pull up the cloves when they have not yet rooted. Keep garlic consistently moist throughout the growing season, to avoid the development of rust on the leaves, which will prematurely cease the development of the bulbs – but be aware of overwatering because garlic will rot if too wet. Harvest bulbs once the leaves have yellowed.

GROWING TIP

Leaving garlic in a dry sunny spot once it has been harvested will help it dry thoroughly and last longer in storage, all the way through the festive season to be enjoyed on the winter plate (see Festive winter vegetables, page 124).

Family
Amaryllidaceae
Height
40cm/16in
Spacing
15cm/6in<>plants;
30cm/12in<>rows
Hardiness
Hardy
Position
Full sun
Edible parts
Bulbs, leaves, flower
stalks, flowers
Harvest
Mid–late summer

GLADIATOR GARLIC
There is evidence that Roman gladiators ate raw garlic before combat as it was thought to give them extra strength during the fight.

SOFTNECK OR HARDNECK?

Garlic is divided into hardneck and softneck varieties. Hardneck ones tend to grow a flower stalk called a scape, which is edible, and these varieties do not store for a long time. Softneck varieties do not tend to flower but do store for much longer after harvesting. Hardneck garlic requires a period of cold, 0°C/32°F to −3°C/27°F, to trigger bulbs to form, a process known as vernalization – overwintered garlic will usually experience such a temperature. Hardnecks also tend to have bigger cloves, although they produce fewer cloves than softnecks.

EDIBLE SCAPES AND WET GARLIC

Garlic scapes are the flower stalks of hardneck varieties and are a delicious treat. It is best horticultural practice to remove scapes before they flower to prevent the garlic from putting too much energy into reproduction. Harvest them by cutting off at their bases as soon as they appear; eat them raw or lightly fried. If the scapes are allowed to develop, the flower can be cut off and eaten.

Immature bulbs harvested before the cloves have fully formed are called wet garlic. This is done at the beginning of the new growing season, and the stem is also edible at this point.

NOTABLE CULTIVARS
Hardneck type
- *A. ampeloprasum* 'Elephant' is a form of leek, but is grown like garlic and produces very large bulbs.
- 'Lautrec Wight' has a delicious taste.
- 'Red Duke' is a red-cloved garlic with a strong flavour.

Softneck type
- 'Early Wight' matures early and is harvestable in early summer.
- 'Germidour' is a purple-skinned variety with a mild flavour.

American groundnut

Apios americana aka potato bean

American groundnut is a vine that produces pretty pink flowers and edible tubers that have a slightly nutty flavour.

—

WHERE TO GROW
Needs a sunny, sheltered spot and a support to climb up throughout the season. Give as much sun as possible although American groundnut tolerates light shade.

HOW TO GROW
Grow from seed tubers, which can be saved from the previous harvest. Either store *in situ*, allowing the plant to regrow in spring, or place in sand over winter and plant out in spring. Cover with a layer of mulch and provide supports for the groundnut to grow up (see Natural supports for broad beans, page 128). Keep this crop consistently watered throughout the growing season.

GROWING TIP
American groundnut can be grown in a large pot as an attractive climber on a patio.

Family	Fabaceae
Height	1.5m/5ft
Spacing	30cm/12in<>plants; 30cm/12in<>rows
Hardiness	Tender; tubers will overwinter in milder areas
Position	Full sun
Edible parts	Tubers, seeds, seed pods
Harvest	Autumn

GONE BUT NOT FORGOTTEN
Although not commonly grown in the UK, this crop was considered as a replacement for the potato in 1845, when Ireland experienced its infamous Potato Famine.

Celery

Apium graveolens

Celery has a distinctive taste and can be cropped over a long season, with the stems being eaten raw or added to cooked dishes. White, green and pink cultivars bring a range of options when choosing which celery to grow (see also Using vegetables as a decorative display, page 54).

—

WHERE TO GROW
Needs moisture-retentive soil, with plenty of organic matter worked in. Celery prefers full sun but tolerates light shade.

HOW TO GROW
Sow under cover in early spring in a seed tray, giving a heat of 15°C/59°F and keeping the compost moist. Seed can take up to three weeks to germinate; once large enough, prick out into modules. Slowly harden off ready for planting in the final position. If growing a self-blanching cultivar, simply transplant and mulch well to retain moisture. If growing a trenching variety, plant into a trench 30cm/12in deep, which will slowly backfill through the growing season or, if growing on flat ground, earth up the celery throughout summer.

GROWING TIP
Keep celery moist throughout the growing season, as in the wild it is a marshland plant.

Family	
Apiaceae	
Height	
40cm/16in	
Spacing	
25cm/10in<>plants;	
25cm/10in<>rows	
Hardiness	
Hardy	
Position	
Full sun	
Edible parts	
Stems, leaves	
Harvest	
Autumn	

NOTABLE CUILTIVARS
- 'Giant Red' has a red stem and is a trenching variety.
- 'Golden Self-blanching', a heritage cultivar developed in Paris in the 1860s, produces pale green stems.
- 'Victoria' is a reliable, self-blanching variety.

A WINNING HARVEST
Celery was an important plant in Ancient Greece, with the plant being part of many rituals and being associated with the cult of the dead. It was also what the winner's wreaths were made from at the Isthmian Games, which were held in honour of Poseidon.

Celeriac

Apium graveolens subsp. *rapaceum*

Although not the most attractive plant in the vegetable garden, celeriac is a winter root vegetable that brings a strong celery flavour to the plate.

—

WHERE TO GROW
Grow in fertile, moisture-retentive soil, adding organic matter in drier sites. Celeriac prefers a sunny site but tolerates light shade.

HOW TO GROW
Celeriac takes a long time to mature, so start in spring for a harvest in autumn. Sow in a seed tray and place in a heat of 15°C/59°F; this crop will take around three weeks to germinate. Prick out into modules and slowly harden off. Plant out once there is little risk of frosts. (Although, when mature, celeriac can survive a light frost, it can stress young plants.) Water in well and mulch to retain the moisture. Ensure this crop is kept moist for a good harvest.

GROWING TIP
Remove lower leaves as they begin to split. This not only improves the appearance of the celeriac root, but also stops the leaves rotting on the plant.

Family
Apiaceae
Height
40cm/16in
Spacing
40cm/16in<>plants;
40cm/16in<>rows
Hardiness
Tolerates light frost
Position
Full sun
Edible parts
Stem
Harvest
Autumn

THE WRONG ROOT
Although classified as a root crop, the edible part of the celeriac is the swollen stem, and when harvested the roots are found below the vegetable.

NOTABLE CULTIVARS
- 'Giant Prague', a heritage cultivar, produces large roots.
- 'Prinz' has a notably smoother skin.

Peanut

Arachis hypogaea

Once the self-pollinated flowers of this legume have been fertilized, the stalks, or pegs, bend towards the ground, eventually penetrating the soil where the immature fruits then develop. Peanuts are the seeds.

WHERE TO GROW
Grow in a sunny spot with free-draining soil that has plenty of organic matter applied. This crop also grows well in a large pot or under glass for the entire summer.

HOW TO GROW
Sow seed under glass in spring; germination should occur within two weeks. Prick out the seedlings into pots and allow to grow until there is little chance of frost. Then harden off and plant outdoors. Once the flowers have formed, ensure the ground below is loose to allow the shoot-like pegs to penetrate it. This crop will generally take around 130 days to harvest, so give it as long a season as possible.

GROWING TIP
Shell and soak seeds for twelve hours before sowing to break down the seed walls and increase the likelihood of germination.

Family	
Fabaceae	
Height	
30cm/12in	
Spacing	
45cm/18in<>plants;	
45cm/18in<>rows	
Hardiness	
Tender	
Position	
Full sun	
Edible parts	
Seeds	
Harvest	
Autumn	

WHAT IS IN A NAME?
Peanuts were named by the botanist Carl Linnaeus, and their species name *hypogaea* means 'under the earth', describing where the seeds develop.

NOTABLE CULTIVARS
• 'Early Spanish' is early maturing and takes 100 days to crop.

Asparagus

Asparagus officinalis

A highlight of spring are the edible spears of asparagus
– one of the first new crops of the season. If not cut,
the spears of this perennial plant grow throughout the
season, becoming tall with wispy foliage and adding
drama to the vegetable garden.
—

WHERE TO GROW

As a perennial vegetable, asparagus needs a permanent
home and does not like to be moved. Give it free-draining
soil in the most sheltered spot in the vegetable
garden with as much sun as possible (see
Creating an asparagus bed, page 46).

HOW TO GROW

The best way to start an asparagus bed is
with crowns in autumn or spring,
although seed can be used
instead. If starting from seed,
sow indoors in late winter,
growing plants in pots to plant
in situ in the following autumn.
Harvest asparagus regularly
throughout spring, then allow
the remaining spears to grow
and 'fern out' so they store
energy for next year's crop.
Give asparagus a good feed
with a balanced granular
fertilizer once cropping has
finished, then lightly mulch
with organic matter in autumn,
being careful not to smother
the crowns.

Family
Asparagaceae
Height
1.5m/5ft
Spacing
30cm/12in<>plants;
30cm/12in<>rows
Hardiness
Hardy
Position
Full sun
Edible parts
Stems
Harvest
Spring

GROWING TIP

A male hybrid such as 'Gijnlim' will produce bigger spears. Female plants produce red berries in autumn, which are fantastic for wildlife, but put a lot of energy into reproduction and therefore give smaller spears, so if looking for a more productive harvest remove these plants.

SUPER SPEARS

Asparagus is an incredibly healthy food and contains no fat or cholesterol. It has also been used as a staple in the medical cabinet, and the Ancient Greeks used it against many ailments including toothache and bee stings.

NOTABLE CULTIVARS

- 'Connovers Colossal' is a heritage variety that has been grown since the 1800s.
- Crimson Pacific' has purple flesh and a good yield.
- 'Gijnlim' is an all-male cultivar that produces large green spears.

Creating an asparagus bed

Asparagus, along with other perennial vegetables, are extremely valuable crops in the vegetable garden as they provide food early in the season and are also expensive to buy in the shops.

Establishing an asparagus bed may take a little patience as the plants cannot be cropped for the first year, and then only a few shoots in the second year. But once the plants are harvestable in their third year, they will continue to crop for more than twenty years. As an asparagus bed is a long-term commitment, the site must be chosen well and have full sun and good access for harvesting, because the crowns do not like to be moved. The bed needs to be weed-free as asparagus crowns are very close to the soil surface and close together, making hoeing awkward. If there are perennial weeds, these will be particularly hard to eradicate once the bed is established, so spending a year removing such weeds and their roots will pay off in the long term.

Asparagus is a coastal plant so needs free-draining soil; it dislikes sitting in waterlogged ground as this may cause the crowns to rot. If the soil retains too much water, dig in grit to improve the area. Asparagus appreciates fertile soil to help it establish so add a 5cm/2in mulch of manure or organic matter to the ground to give a boost in the first year; apply topdressing once the asparagus is established.

Plant up an asparagus bed in autumn or spring when the ground is warm and welcoming. Keep the bed well watered and weeded during the establishment phase.

1. Dig a trench of 20cm/8in deep and 30cm/12in wide, piling the soil to one side of the trench. Add a layer of manure to the bottom and mix with the dug-out soil.
2. Backfill until the trench is around 10cm/4in deep, then create a ridge in the centre of this space, which just comes up to soil level.
3. Place the crowns on the centre of the ridge, encouraging the roots over the sides and ensuring the tops of the crowns are 30cm/12in away from each other and just above soil level.
4. Backfill taking care not to damage the roots; then securely firm the soil.
5. Water well to ensure the roots and soil make contact. Then mulch with compost or manure.

Beetroot

Beta vulgaris

Beetroot is an extremely versatile crop, with the leaves, stems and swollen roots being edible and growing in a range of colours from orange to red to striped pink (see Using vegetables as a decorative display, page 54).

WHERE TO GROW

Grow in a sunny position. Where space is limited, beetroot can be grown in between slow-growing plants such as Brussels sprouts (see page 59). It is also suitable as a windowsill salad (see page 104).

HOW TO GROW

Beetroot can be sown into modules and started under cover in early spring, which will extend the growing season. Sow seeds directly once the soil has warmed to 5°C/41°F and sow in succession for a continuous harvest until late summer or eight weeks before the first frost is predicted. After harvesting, beetroot is best eaten fresh or stored in a root clamp (see page 80).

GROWING TIP

Harvesting the lower leaves throughout the growing season will give you a tasty crop and not damage the beetroot itself.

Family	
Amaranthaceae	
Height	
40cm/16in	
Spacing	
30cm/12in<>plants;	
30cm/12in<>rows	
Hardiness	
Tolerates light frost	
Position	
Full sun	
Edible parts	
Leaves, stems, root	
Harvest	
Spring–autumn	

NOTABLE CULTIVARS

- 'Boltardy' has been bred to minimize bolting; is good for early sowings.
- 'Bull's Blood', a heritage cultivar, produces dark red, edible leaves.
- 'Burpee's Golden' has a warm yellow root, which adds colour to the plate.
- 'Chioggia' has striped pink and white rings when cut.

SWEET BEET

A subspecies of *Beta vulgaris* is sugar beet, which has an extremely high concentration of sucrose. This crop was developed in the mid-eighteenth century and is still a source of sugar today.

Chard

Beta vulgaris Cicla Group

Chard, with its stems ranging from pure white to warm yellow and vivid pink, is a colourful addition to the vegetable garden or border (see Using vegetables as a decorative display, page 54). Both the leaves and stems are long-cropping edibles.

—

WHERE TO GROW

When given moisture-retentive soil with plenty of sun chard thrives, although it does tolerate dappled shade.

HOW TO GROW

Sow seed in modules in mid-spring through to late summer or directly into the ground once the soil temperature has reached 5°C/41°F. If sowing in modules, plant out once roots have filled the module, water in well and mulch. The leaves can be picked when young, or let them mature and enjoy the colourful stems at the same time. Harvest the outside stems from several plants in order to have months of flavour to pick.

GROWING TIP

Late summer sowings of chard can be overwintered and cropped in early spring, which will be a welcome crop during the hungry gap.

Family
Amaranthaceae
Height
60cm/24in
Spacing
30cm/12in<>plants;
30cm/12in<>rows
Hardiness
Hardy
Position
Full sun
Edible parts
Leaves, stems
Harvest
Year-round

NOTABLE CULTIVARS
- 'Bright Lights' produces a vivid mix of stem colours.
- 'Perpetual Spinach' is grown more for its leaf than its stems.
- 'Rhubarb Chard' has red stems.

CLUSTERS OF CHARD
The seed of chard is actually a cluster of several seeds, and therefore sowing one seed will give you three to five plants.

Swede

Brassica × napus aka rutabaga

This root vegetable in the brassica family has a purple tinge to its skin, and is extremely hardy, providing a fresh crop throughout winter.

—

WHERE TO GROW

Needs an open, sunny site and free-draining, light soil, which does not get too wet in winter.

HOW TO GROW

Sow directly into the vegetable garden or start in modules if space is limited. Sow in mid- to late summer, to produce a crop big enough to withstand winter. If using modules, harden off and transplant as soon as possible after germination otherwise the final root may be stunted. Harvest swedes when they reach around 15cm/6in wide.

GROWING TIP

If growing swedes in an area that suffers from long periods of frozen ground or particularly wet winters, it may be best to dig up and store them in a cool root cellar or clamp over winter (see Building a root clamp, page 80), especially if you want to access them for festive occasions (see Festive winter vegetables, page 124).

Family	
Brassicaceae	
Height	
30cm/12in	
Spacing	
30cm/12in<>plants;	
30cm/12in<>rows	
Hardiness	
Hardy	
Position	
Full sun	
Edible parts	
Root	
Harvest	
Autumn–winter	

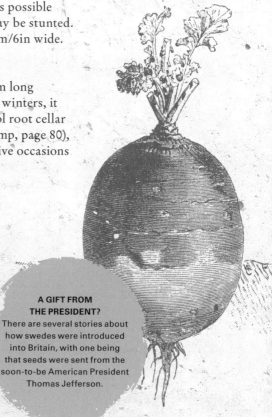

A GIFT FROM THE PRESIDENT?
There are several stories about how swedes were introduced into Britain, with one being that seeds were sent from the soon-to-be American President Thomas Jefferson.

NOTABLE CULTIVARS
- 'Magres' is reliable and gives uniform roots.
- 'Ruby' has red skin and yellow flesh.

Kale

Brassica oleracea Acephala Group

Kale has long been cultivated for its delicious edible leaves. Over winter months they are a welcome addition to the plate (see Festive winter vegetables, page 124) and in summer this crop can be grown as a baby leaf. Most varieties are tall and look striking in the vegetable garden, with a variety of colours and leaf shapes (see Using vegetables as a decorative display, page 54).

WHERE TO GROW

Grow in a sheltered spot with a free-draining soil, especially if it is to be overwintered. Kale tolerates some shade, but the more sun it receives the better the harvest will be, especially over winter. It is also suitable as a windowsill salad (see page 104).

HOW TO GROW

Sow from mid- to late summer to produce plants that will withstand and crop throughout winter. Start off in a seed tray and prick out into larger pots. Allow the roots to fill these pots before hardening off and planting outdoors. Stake taller varieties when planting out (see Natural supports for broad beans, page 128), and ensure roots are firmed in well.

GROWING TIP

Harvest the lowest leaves first to keep the kale plant growing. Kale does not grow quickly once the cold weather sets in, so just harvest a little from each plant as and when it is needed.

Family
Brassicaceae
Height
90cm/36in
Spacing
60cm/24in<>plants;
50cm/20in<>rows
Hardiness
Hardy
Position
Full sun, sheltered
Edible parts
Leaves
Harvest
Winter

A WALKING CROP
Jersey walking stick kale was cultivated in the Channel Isles and can be as tall as 5.5m/18ft. Its thick stem was dried, varnished and used a walking stick.

NOTABLE CULTIVARS
- 'Dwarf Green Curled' produces curled, rich green leaves; grows 60cm/24in tall.
- 'Nero Di Toscana' has dark green leaves.
- 'Redbor' F1 is very ornamental, with red leaves.

TYPES OF PERENNIAL KALE

Some cultivars of kale are perennial and can be harvested year-round. They crop well for around three years and can then easily be replaced by taking cuttings and striking new plants. Notable cultivars include 'Taunton Deane' and 'Daubentons'; acquire these as plants rather than seed to ensure they come true.

Curly kale has an extremely curly and frizzy leaf, with a peppery flavour. The leaf colour comes in a variety of shades from bright green to red. To add a little confusion, there is a fantastic cultivar called 'East Friesian Palm Kale', which is a curly kale that grows over 2m/7ft tall. It is extremely ornamental and looks impressive in a mixed border.

Lacinto kale (aka Tuscan kale, palm kale or dinosaur kale) has a blistered leaf (unlike curly kale) and is much flatter in texture, being similar to a palm leaf. The most well-known cultivar is 'Cavolo Nero', which translates as 'black cabbage' and has a dark green leaf.

Calabrese

Brassica oleracea Botrytis Group

Calabrese can be grown year-round but is at its best in early summer or autumn. The dark green heads are delicious raw or cooked.

—

WHERE TO GROW

Needs a sheltered spot and fertile soil, so apply organic matter to soils that have had heavy feeding crops growing previously or do not retain nutrients, such as sandy soils. Although the plants tolerate some shade, they should have as much light as possible.

HOW TO GROW

Sow in modules in late winter or early spring with some heat or again in late summer. Prick out seedlings into small pots and slowly harden off to plant out in late spring once the roots have filled their pots. Plants can be protected with horticultural fleece if extremely cold temperatures are predicted in spring.

GROWING TIP

Once the main head of calabrese is harvested, a second crop of smaller heads will form if the plant is left in the ground.

Family
Brassicaceae
Height
60cm/24in
Spacing
40cm/16in<>plants;
40cm/16in<>rows
Hardiness
Hardy
Position
Full sun
Edible parts
Florets, leaves
Harvest
Summer–autumn

CALABRESE OR BROCCOLI?
Calabrese is often referred to as broccoli, but calabrese is one large edible inflorescence whereas broccoli is harvested as individual spears.

NOTABLE CULTIVARS
- 'Belstar' produces heads that are slightly slower to run to seed.
- 'Fiesta' is reliable, with dark green heads.

Using vegetables as a decorative display

Vegetables come in a variety of textures, shapes and colours and can be used for interesting decorative or bedding displays. There is a tradition of this at the Royal Botanic Gardens, Kew, where the entire decorative scheme around the Palm House and other areas has been composed of vegetables. Today there are still areas planted in a bedding style but completely composed of edible plants.

The difference between using vegetables for bedding and planting a vegetable garden is that all the crops for the display need to be ready for transplanting at the same time, and the plant spacings are often a little narrower so there is as little visible soil as possible. It is best to start all plants in modules or to purchase plug plants, to make an impact straight away, ensure a neat scheme and be able to plant the entire area all at the once because access can be tricky once the crops fill out.

Decorative displays work best when thoroughly planned. Measure the area and transfer measurements on to squared paper. Work out the spacings and number of plants required, sowing or purchasing around 20 per cent more than needed to give a full and attractive display. Introduce a variety of leaf textures and heights, using crops such as kale and climbing plants plus their supports as dot plants. Choose crops with bright colours such as purple French beans and red-leaved beetroot to go with the backdrop of relaxing greens, which the vegetable garden gives freely.

The decorative display will probably need changing once in midsummer, to keep it looking lush and before the vegetables run to seed. Crops that are fantastic in early displays include broad beans, peas, radishes, red cabbages and beetroot. For the warmer months, tomatoes, peppers and courgettes bring a hit of warmth and texture. Some vegetables including lettuce, chard, carrots and kale work well in all seasons.

1. Prepare the ground thoroughly, removing weeds and creating a fine tilth and a level surface with no dips. Then bring out the plants.
2. Mark out the lines or areas where the different crops will go, using a string line, sand or specialist spray paint.
3. Transplant the young plants into their final positions, laying out before planting if needed; ensure they are firmed in well and watered.
4. Keep weed-free throughout the growth period. Also liquid feed and water. Watch for plants that are not growing well, and replace them with spare plants if necessary.
5. In midsummer, remove the spring scheme and plant summer–autumn crops. There will be a glut of crops, which friends and relatives are sure to enjoy.

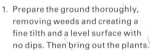

Cauliflower

Brassica oleracea Botrytis Group

Cauliflowers florets come in a range of colours from white to orange and can be cultivated year-round (see Using vegetables as a decorative display, page 54).

WHERE TO GROW
Needs a sheltered spot, and plants staked if it is windy. Grow in an neutral to slightly acidic soil of about pH 6.8, although, if clubroot is an issue on the site, applying an alkali such as lime to the soil will deter this disease and the cauliflowers will be healthier.

HOW TO GROW
Sow in modules in late winter, pricking out into pots and finally hardening off to plant outdoors. Plant this crop slightly deeper than the nursery line and firm roots in extremely well. It is often wise to use a cabbage collar to avoid root fly, and netting against pigeons and cabbage white butterfly will be beneficial (see Troubleshooting, pages 132–4, and Protecting vegetables, page 25). Cauliflowers can also be started in midsummer for an autumn harvest.

GROWING TIP
For the perfect cauliflower look out for the point when the curds form and start to become uneven. Then harvest as soon as possible because curds will run to flower quickly.

Family
Brassicaceae
Height
60cm/24in
Spacing
60cm/24in <>plants;
60cm/24in<>rows
Hardiness
Hardy
Position
Full sun
Edible parts
Florets, leaves
Harvest
Summer–autumn

NOTABLE CULTIVARS
- 'All the Year Round' is reliable; is especially good in spring and summer.
- 'Nine Star Perennial' broccoli is actually a cauliflower; this perennial produces many small curds, and has a similar growth habit to sprouting broccoli (see page 61).
- 'Winter Aalsmeer' is a good overwintering cultivar to harvest in spring.

WHITE AS SNOW
Keep cauliflowers as white as possible by covering each head with their leaves while it is developing. This stops damage from rain and debris.

Cabbage

Brassica oleracea Capitata Group

Cabbages can be produced year-round if a variety of cultivars are grown. They are most welcomed in early summer, as the hungry gap comes to a close, and throughout winter when there is not an abundance of other crops (see also Festive winter vegetables, page 124). They come in many different shapes and colours and textures, adding variety to the vegetable garden (see Using vegetables as a decorative display, page 54).

WHERE TO GROW
Grow in full sun in fertile soil, which is well-drained, especially for overwintering heads. Needs to have as much shelter as possible because the roots do not like to be rocked.

HOW TO GROW
Cabbages can be sown year-round, depending on the cultivar and desired season of harvest (see Types of cabbage, page 58). The aim with plants to be overwintered is to get them large enough so that they can withstand the cold, but are not forming heads, before the first frosts.

Start seed off in a shallow tray, pricking into modules once large enough. Harden off well before planting out, especially those sown in winter. Plant into their final positions, firming roots well into the ground, and water well. Cabbage collars and netting will protect from pests (see Troubleshooting, pages 132–4, and Protecting vegetables, page 25). Earth up the stems to help provide stability in open sites.

GROWING TIP
Cabbages can be fairly slow growing, so interplant with radishes (see page 107) or turnips (see page 62) to optimize the growing space. They can also be interplanted with nasturtium (*Tropaeolum majus*), which can used as a sacrificial crop for caterpillars (see Companion planting, page 25).

Family	
Brassicaceae	
Height	
50cm/20in	
Spacing	
50cm/20in<>plants;	
50cm/20in<>rows	
Hardiness	
Hardy	
Position	
Full sun	
Edible parts	
Leaves	
Harvest	
Year-round	

THE CROSS
Cabbages, along with all other brassicas, now reside in the family Brassicaceae. Originally this family was named Cruciferae due to the flowers produced by brassicas. These have four petals in a cross shape, which medieval Europeans thought resembled a crucifix.

TYPES OF CABBAGE

Spring cabbages will have been overwintered and tend to be small but delicious. When sown in late summer, these can be harvested at any point but are most welcome in the hungry gap in late spring.

Summer cabbages are sown in winter or early spring. They tend to be a sweetheart or hispi, with their heads growing in a conical shape. They are sweeter than most cabbages but will not survive a harsh winter.

Winter cabbages, for harvesting throughout winter, tend to have large heads often with savoy-type leaves, which are blistered in texture. Sow in midsummer so plants have a chance to get to full size before the onset of winter.

NOTABLE CULTIVARS

Spring type
- 'Durham Early' has a sweetheart shape and pale green leaves.

Summer type
- 'Greyhound' is sweetheart shaped, reliable and pale green-leaved.
- 'Kalibos' is a red cabbage with a sweetheart shape.

Winter type
- 'January King', a very hardy heritage savoy variety, living through temperature of −10°C/14°F, produces blue-green leaves.
- 'Tundra' develops a crinkled, ball-shaped head.

Brussels sprout

Brassica oleracea Gemmifera Group

Although sprouts are synonymous with the festive period (see Festive winter vegetables, page 124), this hardy crop is delicious throughout winter, and its tall spires add interest to the vegetable garden in the quiet months.
—

WHERE TO GROW

Requires as much sun as possible in a sheltered position with free-draining soil. Like most brassicas, it needs fertile soil.

HOW TO GROW

For a winter harvest, sow in late spring into modules under glass and allow to get to a good size before hardening off and planting out. Plant slightly above the nursery line and firm in well, providing stakes for support (see Natural supports for broad beans, page 128). Keep this crop consistently watered throughout summer.

As the plant matures, the lower leaves will start to yellow. Remove these by snapping them off to avoid damage to the sprouts. Harvest when the sprouts are 2–3cm/¾–1¼in across, throughout winter.

GROWING TIP

As well as the sprouts, the leaves growing at the top of the plant make a tasty harvest.

Family
Brassicaceae
Height
80cm/32in
Spacing
60cm/24in<>plants;
60cm/24in<>rows
Hardiness
Hardy
Position
Full sun
Edible parts
Sprouts, leaves
Harvest
Winter

SPROUTS × KALE
A recent addition to the brassica range are flower sprouts, a cross between Brussels sprouts and kale, where the sprouts open out to resemble small kale heads.

NOTABLE CULTIVARS
- 'Red Bull' produces red sprouts.
- 'Trafalgar' is extremely reliable.

Kohl rabi

Brassica oleracea Gongylodes Group aka German turnip

Kohl rabi is a swollen stem vegetable in the brassica family. It has a delicate hint of the typical mustard brassica flavour, and is delicious eaten raw or lightly cooked.

—

WHERE TO GROW
Grow in free-draining, preferably sandy soil, giving this crop as much sun as possible.

HOW TO GROW
Sow in spring for an early summer crop, and from late summer to early autumn for a crop to be harvested until mid-winter. Sow indoors or directly into the ground when the soil is at more than 10°C/50°F. If starting indoors, grow in modules and plant out when seedlings are still quite small. Once in their final growing positions, keep kohl rabi well watered to prevent woodiness. Harvest when the stem is the size of a tennis ball.

GROWING TIP
The purple forms are hardier than the green cultivars, so favour the former for later sowings.

Family	Brassicaceae
Height	30cm/12in
Spacing	25cm/10in<>plants; 25cm/10in<>rows
Hardiness	Hardy
Position	Full sun
Edible parts	Stem, leaves
Harvest	Summer, autumn–winter

NOTABLE CULTIVARS
- 'Delicacy White' has pale green skin and white flesh.
- 'Kolibri' is a reliable purple form.

CABBAGE – TURNIP
The name kohl rabi stems from the German words for cabbage, *Kohl*, and turnip, *Rübe*, and it is also sometimes called the German turnip.

Sprouting broccoli

Brassica oleracea Italica Group

A much-needed harvest throughout winter is provided by sprouting broccoli, which adds a purple or white flourish to the vegetable plot and dinner plate (see Festive winter vegetables, page 124).

Family	
Brassicaceae	
Height	
90cm/36in	
Spacing	
60cm/24in<>plants;	
60cm/24in<>rows	
Hardiness	
Hardy	
Position	
Full sun	
Edible parts	
Florets	
Harvest	
Summer, winter	

WHERE TO GROW
Grow in a sheltered spot in fertile, moisture-retentive soil. Stake plants (see Natural supports for broad beans, page 128). Add organic matter to the soil area before planting to get the best harvests.

HOW TO GROW
This crop takes around nine months to come to maturity, so sow in modules under cover in late spring for a winter crop. Once germinated and roots begin to show at the bottom of each module, prick out each seedling and begin hardening off in preparation for transplanting outdoors. Sprouting broccoli dislikes root disturbance so ensure the plants are firmed in well. Keep well watered during hot periods in summer.

GROWING TIP
Harvest the broccoli spears as they appear, to stop them running to seed. This practice also encourages more spears.

COOL TRIGGERS
Sprouting broccoli needs a period of several weeks with temperature below 10°C/50°F to begin forming harvestable spears. This process is called vernalization.

NOTABLE CULTIVARS
- 'Bordeaux' produces purple spears without the vernalization period so can be cropped over summer.
- 'Burbank' F1 has white spears.
- 'Red Spear' is a high-yielding winter variety.

Turnip

Brassica rapa

This fast-growing crop is best enjoyed in early summer or autumn. Its swollen roots come in different colours and shapes (see Using vegetables as a decorative display, page 54), and can be eaten raw or cooked, as can its leaves.

—

WHERE TO GROW

Grow in a sunny site with free-draining soil, applying organic matter to the site for the best harvest. Turnips grow well in pots, too.

HOW TO GROW

Sow in modules or directly into the final position either in spring for an early summer harvest or in autumn for an early winter harvest. Keep the seed compost or soil moist while germination takes place. If starting in modules, transplant turnips when still small. Harvest after 10–12 weeks. After harvesting, turnips are best eaten fresh or stored in a root clamp (see page 80).

GROWING TIP

Turnips are extremely fast growing so can be used as a catch crop (see Succession/Intercropping/Catch cropping, page 24) among slower-growing vegetables such as Brussels sprouts (see page 59).

Family
Brassicaceae
Height
30cm/12in
Spacing
20cm/8in<>plants;
20cm/8in<>rows
Hardiness
Hardy
Position
Full sun
Edible parts
Root, leaves
Harvest
Early summer, early winter

NOTABLE CULTIVARS
- 'Golden Ball' is a globe variety with yellow skin.
- 'Purple Top Milan', a heritage cultivar, has a flat shape and purple shoulders fading to a white root.

COAT OF ARMS
At Hohensalzburg Castle in Salzburg, you will see turnips everywhere, because Archbishop Keutschach decided that his coat of arms would include this crop. Two stories circulate as to why this might be. One is that it symbolized a moment from his childhood when he refused to work, and had a turnip thrown at his head, reminding him of his social responsibility. The other is that it represents the agricultural heritage of his family.

Pak choi

Brassica rapa subsp. *chinensis*

A type of Chinese cabbage that does not form a head, pak choi is cultivated for its stems and mature leaves as well as its baby leaves for salads.

—

WHERE TO GROW
Thrives in full sun with moisture-retentive soil, but will tolerate some shade, especially in very hot summers.

HOW TO GROW
Sow in modules in early spring for an early summer harvest or in late summer for an autumn crop. Pak choi needs 21°C/70°F for good germination, after which grow it at a slightly cooler temperature, of 13–21°C/55–70°F, to avoid bolting. Harden off and transplant seedlings once they are large enough, watering in well. Pak choi can be harvested at any stage of maturity.

GROWING TIP
Baby heads of pak choi can be ready for harvest within thirty days, making it an excellent catch crop (see Succession/Intercropping/Catch cropping, page 24).

Family	Brassicaceae
Height	20cm/8in
Spacing	10cm/4in <>plants; 30cm/12in <>rows
Hardiness	Hardy
Position	Full sun
Edible parts	Stems, leaves
Harvest	Summer–autumn

PEST DEFENCE
Like many brassicas, pak choi contains glucosinolates, which give that distinctive brassica taste through the mustard oils. These oils are released when the plants are damaged and help defend the plant from pest attacks.

NOTABLE CULTIVARS
- 'Canton Dwarf' is compact, with green leaves.
- *B. rapa* var. *rosularis* 'Tatsoi' has dark green leaves in a lat rosette arrangement.

Mizuna

Brassica rapa var. *nipposinica* aka Japanese mustard greens

This brassica leaf crop can be eaten raw or lightly cooked. It adds a mustard taste to any salad and can be cropped as microgreens, baby leaves or large leaves, making it incredibly versatile.

—

WHERE TO GROW
Prefers a sunny position in the vegetable garden, but tolerates light shade. Mizuna can be grown as baby greens and microgreens in a container on a windowsill at any time of year.

HOW TO GROW
Although mizuna can be grown year-round, summer crops tend to bolt. Therefore, sow seed in late summer for an autumn to spring harvest. Start in modules, or directly in the soil. If growing in modules, harden off and transplant when large enough to handle; water in well. If direct-sowing, sow in a drill and thin plants to 10cm/4in, remembering to eat the thinnings.

GROWING TIP
Mizuna can be overwintered outdoors, but it needs some protection from horticultural fleece or a cloche (see Protecting vegetables, page 25).

Family
Brassicaceae
Height
20cm/8in
Spacing
10cm/4in <>plants;
25cm/10in <>rows
Hardiness
Hardy
Position
Full sun
Edible parts
Leaves
Harvest
Autumn–spring

WATER GREENS
The name mizuna comes from the Japanese words *mizu* meaning 'water' and *nu* meaning 'mustard plant'. The name refers to the flooded fields that this crop is sometimes grown in.

Komatsuna

Brassica rapa var. *perviridis*

Being a member of the brassica family, this leafy vegetable provides that characteristic mustard flavour throughout the seasons.

—

WHERE TO GROW
Grow winter crops in full sun in free-draining, fertile soil. If grown throughout summer, komatsuna will benefit from light shade, which will stop it from bolting.

HOW TO GROW
For winter crops, sow seeds in late summer in modules. Allow each seedling to fill its module, then harden off and transplant to the final growing site. Water in well. Harvest little and often throughout the cold months.

GROWING TIP
Komatsuna leaves become stronger flavoured as they mature, so for a mild mustard taste harvest them young.

Family	
Brassicaceae	
Height	
30cm/12in	
Spacing	
5cm/2in ◇plants;	
30cm/12in ◇rows	
Hardiness	
Hardy	
Position	
Full sun or partial shade	
Edible parts	
Leaves	
Harvest	
Year-round	

SENPOSAI
This leaf vegetable is a hybrid between komatsuna and cabbage, giving a tender-leaved crop with a sweet cabbage flavour.

Pepper

Capsicum annuum

Peppers are a colourful end-of-summer crop. Coming in a range of heats, from sweet to extremely pungent and hot, the fruits can be eaten raw, cooked or dried for seasoning food.

WHERE TO GROW
Needs a sunny, sheltered spot and fertile, free-draining soil. Grows extremely well in a greenhouse, too.

HOW TO GROW
Peppers need a very long growing season, so sow under glass in a seed tray in late winter, covering with vermiculite. Leave in a temperature of 18–21°C/65–70°F to germinate (this can take up to thirty days) and prick out into modules once the first true leaves start to appear. Transplant into larger pots and slowly harden off to plant in their final positions once there is little risk of frost. Stake plants to prevent damage once they become laden with fruits (see Natural supports for broad beans, page 128).

GROWING TIP
Picking peppers when they are green encourages a higher yield, but allowing fruit to ripen further on the plant increases its distinctive qualities, be it heat or sweetness.

Family
Solanaceae
Height
60cm/24in
Spacing
45cm/18in <>plants;
75cm/30in <>rows
Hardiness
Tender
Position
Full sun
Edible parts
Fruits
Harvest
Late summer–autumn

A PECK OF PEPPERS
As well as *C. annuum*, other species of *Capsicum* are also commonly grown, including *C. frutescens* (which includes Tabasco peppers), *C. pubescens* (which includes Rocoto peppers), *C. chinense* (which includes Habanero peppers) and *C. baccatum*.

NOTABLE CULTIVARS
Chilli peppers
- 'Habanero' produces very hot-fleshed fruit.
- 'Scotch Bonnet' is a small red chilli, which is extremely pungent; originally from the Caribbean.
- 'Tabasco' is a heritage cultivar from 1848; the small fruits change from green to orange to red, and pack a punch.

Sweet peppers
- 'Marconi Rosso' is a sweet variety, with long red fruit.
- 'Padron' is mainly picked when green and is very mild, although one in every ten has some heat.
- 'Tangerine Dream' bears small, sweet, orange fruits with a very slight pungency to them; grows well in a pot.

HOT SAUCE
The heat of a pepper can be assessed against a scale called the Scoville scale, which measures the concentration of capsaicin in units called Scoville Heat Units (SHU). This way of defining heat came from Wilbur Scoville, an American pharmacist, in 1912. A bell pepper has a rating of 0–100 SHU, whereas a Scotch Bonnet pepper has a rating of 100,000–350,000 SHU. The current hottest peppers have SHU ratings of 800,000–3,200,000 and include the Carolina Reaper and the Dragon's Breath pepper (which was developed in the UK).

Endive

Cichorium endivia

This hardy salad crop has harvestable leaves throughout the cold months when given some protection (see Protecting vegetables, page 25).

—

WHERE TO GROW

Needs as much sun as possible and moisture-retentive soil. If grown in summer, endive will tolerate light shade. It does not need high nutrient levels so can follow on from a heavy-feeding crop such as potatoes (see page 121).

HOW TO GROW

Sow in modules in spring for a summer crop or in late summer for an autumn and winter harvest. Harden off and plant out once seedlings have three or four true leaves, then water well. Harvest once endive has hearted up or slowly harvest the outside leaves if growing a looser form such as 'Bianca Riccia da Taglio'.

GROWING TIP

To reduce some of the characteristic bitterness of endive by blanching, cover each head with a bucket for around two weeks before harvesting.

Family
Asteraceae
Height
20cm/8in
Spacing
25cm/10in <>plants;
25cm/10in <>rows
Hardiness
Tolerates light frost
Position
Full sun
Edible parts
Leaves
Harvest
Summer, autumn–winter

WHITE GOLD
Discovered in Belgium in 1830, this crop became known as White Gold in Paris when it was introduced in 1872, because of its popularity.

NOTABLE CULTIVARS
- 'Encornet de Bordeaux', an heirloom variety, is very hardy, surviving down to –5°C/23°F.
- 'Pancalieri' is self-blanching, with curled leaves.

Chicory

Cichorium intybus

A beautiful winter vegetable, chicory leaves can be eaten raw, or the chicons can be cooked after being forced. The root can also be used as a substitute for coffee.

WHERE TO GROW
Needs full sun and free-draining soil for best results. Chicory will tolerate light shade and a less fertile soil than other vegetables.

HOW TO GROW
For an autumn and winter crop, sow seeds in summer. Sow in modules; harden off and plant out once seedlings are large enough. For raddichio and sugarloaf chicories, loose leaves can be harvested whenever required, but the hearts are ready when they are firm to the touch.

To force witloof chicory, dig up the root in autumn, trim the leaves, place the root in a box of moist garden compost and leave in a warm dark place or cover with a bucket, giving a temperature of around 15°C/59°F (see Forced rhubarb, page 110). This will then produce forced buds, or chicons, ready for harvesting.

GROWING TIP
Chicories start life looking like a dandelion (*Taraxacum officinale*; a close relative) but will slowly change colour and growth habit as they mature.

Family	
Asteraceae	
Height	
30cm/12in	
Spacing	
30cm/12in <>plants;	
30cm/12in <>rows	
Hardiness	
Tolerates light frost	
Position	
Full sun	
Edible parts	
Leaves, chicons, roots	
Harvest	
Autumn–winter	

THREE OF THE SAME
Chicory is organized into three types: witloof/Belgian – these produce large edible buds called chicons when forced; raddichio – red-leaved chicory, which hearts up and blanches the centre leaves; sugarloaf – these produce green leaves and upright, self-blanching hearts.

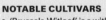

NOTABLE CULTIVARS
- 'Brussels Witloof' is a witloof type and produces chicons when forced.
- 'Pain de Sucre' is a sugarloaf type and resembles a cos lettuce.
- 'Palla Rossa' is a reliable raddichio.

Miner's lettuce

Claytonia perfoliata aka Indian lettuce, spring beauty, winter purslane

This succulent leaf, which is perfect for an autumn harvest, adds an interesting texture to the salad bowl.
—

WHERE TO GROW
Thrives in a free-draining soil in full sun but will also tolerate partial shade.

HOW TO GROW
Sow in modules in late summer, keeping the compost moist throughout germination. Harden off and transplant when plants are large enough to handle, then water well. Harvest the leaves as and when desired. Providing some protection will keep this crop harvestable throughout winter months (see Protecting vegetables, page 25).

GROWING TIP
Miner's lettuce seeds freely, but its seedlings are incredibly distinctive with long leaf stalks and rounded leaves; these can be eaten at this young stage.

Family	
Montiaceae	
Height	
15cm/6in	
Spacing	
15cm/6in <>plants;	
20cm/8in <>rows	
Hardiness	
Tolerates light frost	
Position	
Full sun	
Edible parts	
Leaves	
Harvest	
Autumn–early winter	

A MINER'S REMEDY
The name miner's lettuce originated from the miners in the Californian Gold Rush, who ate it to prevent scurvy. It is rumoured to have been introduced into Europe in 1794 by Archibald Menzies, when he bought it to the Royal Botanic Gardens, Kew.

Seakale

Crambe maritima

This perennial crop grows wild by the coast in Europe and is cultivated for its blanched stems in spring – a welcome delicacy at a time of year when little else is coming from the vegetable garden.

—

WHERE TO GROW

Requires a sunny open site and free-draining soil. As a perennial, it needs several years to develop so be sure to exclude it from rotation beds.

HOW TO GROW

Plant thongs (root cuttings) directly in the soil in spring or start seakale from seed in late winter, surrounded by a heat of 7°C/45°F, eventually planting out in summer. To ensure the soil is free-draining, add grit to each planting hole if required. Remove flowers from seakale to avoid energy being put into reproduction. Do not harvest in the first spring after planting, to allow the plants to mature. The plants will die back over winter, and when they reappear blanch (see Forced rhubarb, page 110) and crop the stems. Mulch and feed with a multipurpose granular fertilizer after harvesting.

GROWING TIP

The reason that the stems of seakale are usually blanched is because this enhances their sweetness. Blanching is done by excluding light and making the stems elongate in their search for a light source. This draws on stored starches for growth, and produces sugars.

Family
Brassicaceae
Height
60cm/24in
Spacing
60cm/24in <>plants;
60cm/24in <>rows
Hardiness
Hardy
Position
Full sun
Edible parts
Stems, leaves
Harvest
Spring

ALL AT SEA
The Romans would eat seakale on long journeys to prevent scurvy; usually it was pickled.

Cucumber

Cucumis sativus

Home-grown cucumbers are a fantastic addition to any salad, and it is a joy to eat the cooling, juicy fruits directly from the plant on a hot day.

—

WHERE TO GROW

Grow outdoors or in the greenhouse, depending on the cultivar. In the greenhouse, give cucumbers a moisture-retentive growing medium and somewhere to grow up (see Natural supports for broad beans, page 128). Outdoors, plant them in the sunniest position available, and give them a trellis to grow up or else enough space to trail.

HOW TO GROW

Sow into 9cm/3½in pots in spring, in surroundings of 20°C/68°F while germination occurs; after this, an optimum growing temperature of 28°C/82°F is required. Harden off and plant out once there is little risk of frost. Add plenty of organic matter to the soil or pot in the greenhouse before planting out the cucumbers. Keep the soil moist throughout the growing season.

GROWING TIP

Pinch out the growing tips when plants reach the desired height, to encourage a bushy form, which in turn encourages more fruits.

Family
Cucurbitaceae
Height
2m/7ft
Spacing
45cm/18in <>plants;
75cm/30in <>rows
Hardiness
Tender
Position
Full sun
Edible parts
Fruits
Harvest
Autumn–early winter

VIRGIN FRUIT
Some cucumbers are parthenocarpic, which means they can fruit without fertilization, leading to a seedless harvest.

NOTABLE CULTIVARS
- 'Crystal Lemon' is a rounded, yellow cultivar introduced around 1894; can be grown outdoors.
- 'Telegraph Improved' is a long, green indoor variety and crops reliably.

Creating a wildlife-friendly vegetable garden

As well as feeding ourselves, the vegetable patch can, with the right planting, provide food for other animals and insects. Many vegetables provide pollen for bees in exchange for pollination. For example, legumes such as peas and beans can be cropped for a long period, thereby providing pollen for a good length of time, from broad beans and peas in late spring, through to runner beans in early autumn. Companion planting with flowers attracts many insects including ladybirds, hoverflies and lacewings as they come to feed off the nectar of plants such as pot marigold (*Calendula officinalis*). These insects will also help to control aphid problems, and the pot marigold petals are a delicious edible.

Avoiding chemical use in the vegetable garden highly benefits wildlife, because the chemicals can easily enter the food chain and have very negative consequences. A prime example of this are slug pellets; once the slug is poisoned, it may still be eaten by birds and hedgehogs. Instead of scattering slug pellets, remove slugs by hand, scatter paper pellets, utilize traps or encourage more natural predators.

Creating a natural hedge gives wildlife places to hide and nest, and if planted with edibles such as blackberries, sloes and roses for hips, this boundary can feed as well as protect.

In addition to wildlife that is visible, remember to nurture those below ground. No-dig cultivation does not disturb the soil, allowing microorganisms to flourish and, because worms do not like to be disturbed, increases populations of these beneficial creatures.

Thus, in the vegetable garden, working with wildlife is a balance as some creatures can become detrimental to crops, but developing a healthy ecosystem and using barrier methods of pest control lend themselves to a more sustainable plot.

A Use flowers (here nasturtium/ *Tropaeolum majus*) for companion planting, to provide insects with nectar. Plants of many different flower shapes will encourage a variety of beneficial insects.

B Allow asparagus to produce berries to give birds a food source in autumn; also leave the heads on globe artichokes.

C Make up some comfrey feed and set up barrier controls and natural methods of pest control where possible, in order to avoid introducing chemicals into the vegetable plot.

D Avoid using slug pellets as these are proven to kill birds; instead try barrier methods such as paper pellets to protect plants.

E Provide water for animals and insects to drinks and bath in. From a pond to a saucer of milk, wildlife will appreciate this addition to the vegetable garden.

Courgette and summer squash

Cucurbita pepo

Courgettes and summer squash are reliable and easy crops to cultivate and find a home for in most vegetable gardens. Courgettes produce long tapered fruits, whereas summer squash vary in shape. The fruits of both vegetables are delicious when small – less than 15cm/6in long – and their flowers are a delicacy in their own right.

WHERE TO GROW
Grow in a sunny spot with moisture-retentive, fertile soil. Plant around the base of climbing plants such as beans to shade the soil and to smother weeds.

HOW TO GROW
Sow under glass in mid- to late spring, or directly in the ground in early summer. If starting under glass, sow into 9cm/3½in pots and provide a temperature of 20°C/68°F for strong germination. Once plants are large enough, harden off and plant out once there is little risk of frost. Ensure plants are kept moist throughout the growing season.

GROWING TIP
Sow a second crop in early summer so that once spring-sown plants begin to slow production in mid- to late summer, the second batch will provide a good harvest into early autumn.

Family
Cucurbitaceae
Height
60cm/24in
Spacing
1m/3ft <>plants;
1m/3ft <>rows
Hardiness
Tender
Position
Full sun
Edible parts
Fruits, flowers
Harvest
Summer–autumn

NOTABLE CULTIVARS
Courgette
• 'Defender' is reliable and has dark green fruits.
• 'Orelia' produces yellow fruits.
Summer squash
• 'Patty Pan' is a scallop-edged squash and comes in a variety of colours.

A NODE ON A SQUASH
The main difference between a winter squash and a summer squash is the length of the internodes. Summer squash have smaller internodes, leading to a bushy habit. Bush forms of *C. pepo* produce fruits sooner, which inhibits vegetative growth.

Winter squash
Cucurbita pepo

Throughout summer, winter squash are absorbing bright colours and flavours and storing them up to be savoured again in the duller winter months (see also Festive winter vegetables, page 124). Coming in a variety of shapes and colours, these tough-skinned fruits often have curious names and histories.

—

WHERE TO GROW
Needs an open, sunny site, and as much fertility as possible. Being trailing plants they need space to spread or to clamber up a strong support (see Natural supports for broad beans, page 128). If space is limited, train plants into spirals and pinch out the growing tip, once the desired number of fruits have formed.

HOW TO GROW
Sow indoors in early spring in 9cm/3½in pots; seeds need a minimum temperature of 13°C/55°F to germinate. Do not sow too early or else plants will be too large before the frost dies away and they can be hardened off and transplanted outdoors. When planting out, add organic matter to each growing hole, to help retain moisture. If soil is particularly free-draining, mulch around each plant, creating a watering well, because these plants like moist roots.

GROWING TIP
Placing slate or tiles under ripening fruits lifts them away from the ground, where there is a chance of rotting. Turning the fruits gently will also ensure an even colour to the skins.

Family
Cucurbitaceae
Height
3m/10ft
Spacing
1m/3ft <>plants;
1.5m/5ft <>rows
Hardiness
Tender
Position
Full sun
Edible parts
Fruits, flowers
Harvest
Autumn

NOTABLE CULTIVARS
- 'Crown Prince' (*C. maxima*) has blue skin and bright orange flesh.
- 'Spaghetti', once cooked, has flesh that gains a spaghetti-like quality.
- 'Uchiki Kuri' is a reliable heavy cropper with orange fruit.

PEPO AND MORE
Although most winter squash are categorized as *C. pepo*, the grouping also includes *C. maxima* (Hubbard squash) and *C. moschata* (butternut squash). The word 'squash' comes from the Native-American term *askutasquash*, meaning eaten raw or uncooked.

Pumpkin

Cucurbita pepo

Pumpkins are synonymous with autumn and Halloween; with their orange skins and sweet flesh they also add a hit of colour in the vegetable garden (see Using vegetables as a decorative display, page 54).

—

WHERE TO GROW

Requires an open, sunny position and fertile soil. Also needs a lot of room to scramble and, if you are growing a large cultivar, good access for harvesting is essential.

HOW TO GROW

Sow in spring in 9cm/3½in pots placed in a temperature of 13–21°C/55–70°F to germinate. The seedlings grow rapidly, so do not start sowing too soon before the last predicted frost date. Once it is ready to be planted out, add organic matter to the area where the pumpkin is to be grown. Mulch around the plant once it has been planted, firmed in and watered well. Apply liquid feed weekly during the flowering period to help flowers to set. Thin fruits, to encourage large pumpkins.

GROWING TIP

To ensure a long storage life for pumpkins, allow them to cure for a week once harvested. This means placing them either on the ground in sunny weather or in a light, dry, protected area, and allowing as much moisture as possible to leave the skin.

Family
Cucurbitaceae
Height
3m/10ft
Spacing
1m/3ft <>plants;
1.5m/5ft <>rows
Hardiness
Tender
Position
Full sun
Edible parts
Fruits, flowers
Harvest
Autumn

NOTABLE CULTIVARS

- 'Atlantic Giant' is the pumpkin of choice if you are trying to grow the biggest for the prize table.
- 'Jack be Little' produces masses of small pumpkins.

JACK O'LANTERN

This nickname has its roots in the phenomenon of lights that sometime appear over peat bogs – most likely caused by the agitation of combustible gas, but historically thought to be spirits. The lights were known as *ignis fatuus* (foolish fire), or Jack-o'-lanterns, based on the folk tale Stingy Jack.

Globe artichoke

Cynara cardunculus subsp. *scolymus*

A perennial crop, artichokes produce delicious edible heads as well as ornamental silver foliage. Such a striking plant works well in a mixed border as well as in the vegetable plot (see Using vegetables as a decorative display, page 54).

—

WHERE TO GROW
Needs free-draining soil because it is winter moisture rather than the cold that is most likely to lead to an unsuccessful crop of globe artichokes. A sheltered, sunny spot is also essential for this crop.

HOW TO GROW
Raise from offsets of existing plants or else sow in late winter and place in a heat of 15°C/59°F to germinate. Once large enough, prick seedlings into pots and allow to grow on until they can be hardened off and planted out. When in their final position, do not allow to dry out in their first summer. While plants are still young, winter protection may be necessary (see Protecting vegetables, page 25). Harvest the flowering buds in late spring or early summer.

GROWING TIP
Although globe artichokes are perennial vegetables, to ensure a constantly fruitful harvest replace a third of the plants every year because they are short-lived and become less productive after their third or fourth year.

Family
Asteraceae
Height
1m/3ft
Spacing
75cm/30in <>plants;
1m/3ft <>rows
Hardiness
Hardy, may require some protection in extreme winters
Position
Full sun
Edible parts
Fruits, flowers
Harvest
Late spring

MARILYN
Castroville in California, USA hosts an annual artichoke festival and claims to be the Artichoke Centre of the World. In 1948, Castroville's Artichoke Queen was a young Marilyn Monroe, then going by her name of Norma Jean.

CYNAR
The bitter liqueur Cynar is flavoured predominantly with artichokes, and is sometimes used to replace Campari in the cocktail negroni.

NOTABLE CULTIVARS
- 'Green Globe' is reliable, with large green heads.
- 'Violet de Provence' has purple heads.

Carrot

Daucus carota subsp. *sativus*

Carrots come in an array of colours from orange, yellow, purple and white, making them a very attractive addition to any plate (see also Festive winter vegetables, page 124). Forcing varieties can be sown at the beginning of the season when the weather is slightly cooler; these tend to be short and stumpy in shape.

—

WHERE TO GROW

When grown in full sun, carrots do best in sandy soil. There is no need to add organic matter to the ground where carrots are to grow as they do not need highly fertile soil, so they do well following on from heavy-feeding crops, which may have depleted the soil.

HOW TO GROW

Directly sow in the ground from late spring to late summer, because transplanting often causes damage to the root, resulting in a stunted crop. Sow thickly in rows to a depth of around 2cm/¾in and gradually thin out to the final 10cm/4in spacing throughout the season. Keep carrot beds weed-free to avoid competition. After harvesting, carrots are best eaten fresh or stored in a root clamp (see page 80).

GROWING TIP

One of the biggest carrot pests is the carrot fly (see Root flies, page 134). Their maggots tunnel into carrot roots, making them vulnerable to rotting. The egg-laying adult flies, which are attracted by the smell of carrot foliage, are low fliers, so erect a 60cm/24in high barrier of very fine netting around the crop to help prevent access.

Family
Apiaceae
Height
40cm/16in
Spacing
10cm/4in <>plants;
30cm/12in <>rows
Hardiness
Tolerates some frost
Position
Full sun, free-draining soil
Edible parts
Root
Harvest
Late spring–Autumn

ALL THE CARROTS OF THE RAINBOW

Originally, carrots were not orange at all, but yellow, purple, red and white – orange carrots appeared only in the sixteenth century. Folklore has it that red and yellow carrots were crossbred to create orange carrots in support of William I of Orange.

TYPES OF CARROT

Amsterdam are early baby carrots, which are fairly narrow and short with stump ends. They can be forced for an early crop and grow in heavy soil.

Berlicum are good for winter growth and have large cylindrical roots.

Chantenay are main-crop and autumn carrots; they are short and broad with a conical shape. They grow in heavy soils and tolerate some frost.

Imperator need free-draining, light soil and store well. They are hardier than other carrot types, and produce a long, tapered root.

Nantes are stump-ended and grown for early and main crops. One of the sweetest types, they do not store well.

Paris Market are French Heritage carrots and are small with a rounded shape. They tolerate heavy soil.

NOTABLE CULTIVARS

Amsterdam type
- 'Amsterdam Forcing' has sweet, orange flesh.

Berlicum type
- 'Bangor' is heavy yielding, with orange flesh.

Chantenay type
- 'Chantenay Red Cored' has a deep red-orange centre and is very sweet.

Imperator type
- 'Autumn King' is one of the largest carrots and produces reliably high yields.

Nantes type
- 'Early Nantes' is one of the earliest and quickest to mature of the Nantes type.

Paris Market type
- 'Atlas' is a small, sweet carrot and grows reliably.

Building a root clamp

Clamps are a way of storing root crops in the vegetable garden, which is useful if space is limited in the home. They were particularly popular on the home front during the Dig for Victory campaign during the Second World War. Clamps are suitable for most root crops including carrots, potatoes, beetroot, turnips and swedes.

Site the clamp in the driest and most sheltered area of the vegetable plot and create it in early autumn, when conditions are still warm. The clamp will have two trenches either side, which drain water away from it. The clamp itself is formed of straw and soil, with sand being placed on the floor of the clamp if extra drainage is needed. Build the store upwards, so that the crops are above the frost level.

When storing the vegetables, save only those in perfect condition with no defects where rot may get in, because rot will spread quickly throughout the clamp. Remove all stalks, stems and leaves – these again will rot in the clamp.

A clamp is taken apart from either end, so pile up a mixture of vegetables or make several different clamps for different crops. The clamp should last until the end of winter unless it is particularly cold and wet, in which case it may be worth checking the crops for deterioration. After dismantling the clamp, add the straw to the compost heap, or use it as mulch, especially around strawberries when they fruit.

1. Dig two parallel trenches, 30cm/12in wide and 1.5m/5ft apart. Pile the soil in the space between the two trenches.
2. Place a layer of straw on to the soil mound, making it thick enough so that the soil cannot be seen.
3. Arrange a single layer of the root vegetables and allow to dry before adding the next layer, slowly creating a pyramidal shape up to around 1m/3ft tall.
4. Cover the top of the clamp with another thick layer of straw, then top with soil. Leave a vent at the top of the clamp, packed with straw to allow airflow.
5. Remove the vegetables as required, starting from one end of the clamp, ensuring that you reseal the open end each time.

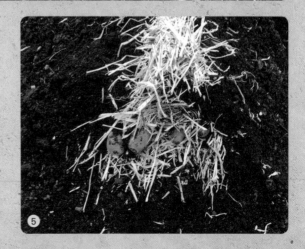

Rocket

Eruca vesicaria aka arugula, salad rocket

This spicy crop has toothed leaves and is part of the brassica family, so it adds heat to a salad bowl.

—

WHERE TO GROW

Needs light shade, to avoid bolting, and moisture-retentive soil. Rocket is also suitable as a windowsill salad (see page 104).

HOW TO GROW

Although rocket can be grown year-round, it is most valuable as an autumn crop and is less likely to run to seed then. It can be sown directly in early spring or late summer, into a shallow drill, thinning plants to 15cm/6in apart. Rocket tends to bolt in high temperatures, so it is only worth sowing in the cooler months. Keep well watered. Harvest when required because rocket will continually put out new leaves. Pull up plants once they run to seed.

GROWING TIP

When given some protection in autumn and winter (see Protecting vegetables, page 25), rocket will crop for a long season.

Family
Brassicaceae
Height
20cm/8in
Spacing
15cm/6in <>plants;
15cm/6in <>rows
Hardiness
Tolerates some frost
Position
Partial shade
Edible parts
Leaves
Harvest
Autumn–early winter

NOTABLE CULTIVARS
- 'Astra' is reliable and produces a true rocket taste.
- 'Fireworks' has red-veined leaves.
- 'Wasabi' has a slight wasabi tang.

MORE CHOICE
As well as the annual *E. vesicaria*, there is also wild rocket (*Diplotaxis tenuifolia*), which has a stronger flavour, and Turkish rocket (*Bunias orientalis*) – both perennials.

Florence fennel

Foeniculum vulgare var. *azoricum* aka bulb fennel

Florence fennel produces a white bulb with feathery foliage and has a fresh aniseed taste. Whether eaten cooked or raw, this vegetable adds a taste of summer to any plate.

—

WHERE TO GROW

Needs full sun and free-draining soil. Because it is sown in midsummer, fennel can take the place of a harvested crop such as beetroot or spring cabbage.

HOW TO GROW

Sow in midsummer, either directly in the ground or in modules. If growing in modules, plant out once each plant has around three true leaves. Water in well, adding a thin layer of mulch around but not touching the stem of each plant. The bulbs will start swelling after around six weeks and are harvestable at any time.

GROWING TIP

Although you can sow fennel in spring, such sowings tend to bolt before producing a bulb. This is because Florence fennel is a long-day plant and produces flowers when the day length is more than thirteen and a half hours.

Family	
Apiaceae	
Height	
50cm/20in	
Spacing	
30cm/12in <>plants;	
30cm/12in <>rows	
Hardiness	
Tender	
Position	
Full sun	
Edible parts	
Bulb	
Harvest	
Late summer–autumn	

FENNEL FIRE
In the Greek myth, Prometheus is said to have stolen fire from the gods and given it to humans by stealing an ember of fire and hiding it in a fennel stalk.

NOTABLE CULTIVARS
- 'Romanesco' produces large white bulbs.
- 'Zefa Fino' was developed to be less prone to bolting, to allow for spring sowings.

Soya bean

Glycine max aka edamame

These beans can be harvested at two different stages of maturity: as edamame, which are the immature green pods; or as soya beans, which are the matured pods when the leaves have started to turn yellow.

—

WHERE TO GROW
Needs a long growing season so plant in the warmest, most sheltered, sunny spot. Free-draining soil with organic matter added will give the best harvest.

HOW TO GROW
In late spring or early summer, soak the seeds for twelve hours prior to sowing to aid germination. Then sow two seeds in each 9cm/3½in pot and set in a propagator or greenhouse. Seeds need a minimum temperature of 14°C/57°F to germinate, which should occur within two weeks. Ensure roots have filled out the pots before planting out.

GROWING TIP
Soya beans will benefit from a boundary support, especially if growing to fully mature soya-bean stage (see Natural supports for broad beans, page 128).

NOTABLE CULTIVARS
- 'Green Shell' has long, dark green pods, each containing around three beans.
- 'Fiskeby V' is a good bean for a cooler climate.

Family
Fabaceae
Height
60cm/24in
Spacing
15cm/6in <>plants;
45cm/18in <>rows
Hardiness
Tender
Position
Full sun
Edible parts
Seed pods, seeds
Harvest
Late summer–autumn

THE BEAN MACHINE
Henry Ford, who created the Ford car company, had a passion for using soya beans as a material in industry. Ideas included using soya fibres in car panels to create a lighter vehicle, and the extraction of oil from the bean to use as a lacquer in car paints.

Jerusalem artichoke

Helianthus tuberosus

A perennial root crop, Jerusalem artichokes have a slight nutty flavour and are an easy crop to grow.

—

WHERE TO GROW

Jerusalem artichokes grow in most free-draining soils and like full sun, but will tolerate some shade. They can also be grown in very large pots. Ensure these very tall plants do not shade out a sun-loving neighbour.

HOW TO GROW

In early spring, plant tubers around 15cm/6in deep and cover with a layer of mulch. Keep moist throughout the season. Cut back the stems once the leaves turn yellow. Harvest as and when required throughout autumn and winter until these perennials begin to grow again in spring.

GROWING TIP

If planting Jerusalem artichokes in an exposed site, earth up the rows when the stems reach 30cm/12in to help to stabilize the plants.

Family
Asteraceae
Height
2.5m/8ft
Spacing
30cm/12in <>plants;
30cm/12in <>rows
Hardiness
Hardy
Position
Full sun
Edible parts
Tubers
Harvest
Autumn–winter

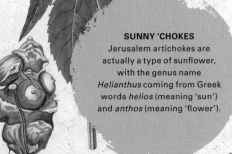

SUNNY 'CHOKES
Jerusalem artichokes are actually a type of sunflower, with the genus name *Helianthus* coming from Greek words *helios* (meaning 'sun') and *anthos* (meaning 'flower').

NOTABLE CULTIVARS
- 'Fuseau' has smooth, white skin.
- 'Gerard' is red skinned.

Sweet potato

Ipomoea batatas aka yam

This trailing vine with its colourful edible tubers, which are adapted underground stems, produces a delicious crop.

—

WHERE TO GROW

Needs fertile, free-draining soil and grows well in sandy soil with additional organic matter. Sweet potatoes require a lot of warmth so plant in the sunniest, most sheltered spot possible. The vine will need either a support to climb up (see Natural supports for broad beans, page 128) or else room to scramble around.

HOW TO GROW

In late winter, start sweet potatoes from slips (cuttings) (see Sweet-potato slips, page 88) or small plants. When slips form in spring, put them into water until roots appear from the base, then pot up into a long tom, keeping moist throughout this period. Harden off and plant out once the soil is fully warmed up in summer, burying the stem into the soil. Keep well watered throughout summer before digging up the tubers in autumn.

GROWING TIP

Once harvested, sweet potatoes should be cured to make them sweet. Curing is the process whereby starches are turned into sugars, and sweet potatoes need a week in humid conditions for this to occur.

Family
Convolvulaceae
Height
20cm/8in
Spacing
30cm/12in ◇plants;
75cm/30in ◇rows
Hardiness
Tender
Position
Full sun
Edible parts
Tubers
Harvest
Autumn

YAM
Sweet potatoes are often referred to as yams, as is *Oxalis tuberosa*, but technically a yam is an edible in the genus *Dioscorea*. The word yam probably derives from the Portuguese *inhame*.

NOTABLE CULTIVARS
- 'Beauregard' has orange flesh and skin.
- 'Carolina Ruby' has dark orange, nearly red flesh.

Sweet-potato slips

Sweet potatoes (*Ipomoea batatas*) can easily be propagated at home from stored tubers. When purchasing sweet-potato plants, what is actually being obtained are sweet-potato slips, or shoots. Slips are the shoots of the sweet potato, which can be broken off, transplanted and will eventually form their own roots. The first stage is to force the tuber to produce vines early in the year, and this process requires heat, preferably from a heat mat set to 21°C/70°F. Each plant will produce roughly 3–5 shoots, but not all of them may root, so it is often worth sprouting several tubers. The sprouting process takes around six weeks, and then the rooting of the slips another month.

To obtain sweet-potato tubers early in the season to create slips from, it is best to store some medium-sized ones over winter, from the previous season's harvest. Store only those with no damage or signs of disease in a dark, cool, pest-free environment. Then in late winter lay the tubers on moist seed compost, to start sprouting. Once the slips have formed and been taken off the parent tuber, place them in water while they develop their own root systems.

Slips are quite long and prefer growing in pots called long toms, which are much longer than normal pots and are often used for climbing plants. The slips need moist but free-draining compost. Once in pots, slips benefit from being fed with high-potassium fertilizer, to encourage further rooting, before being hardened off and planted out.

1. Place the sweet potatoes on their sides into moist compost, half in and half out. Place the pots on a heat mat.
2. The slips will take around six weeks to grow to the desired height of 15cm/6in.
3. Pull the slips off the tuber when ready and remove the lower leaves.
4. Place slips into a clear jar or jug filled with water and set on the heat mat while they develop roots. Change the water every few days.
5. Once the roots have reached 5cm/2in long, transplant into pots and slowly harden off, keeping the soil moist.

Lettuce

Lactuca sativa

Lettuce comes in many shapes, colours and textures. An easy crop to grow, it is incredibly ornamental and can be cultivated on the windowsill (see Windowsill salads, page 104), in a pot or in open ground. See also Using vegetables as a decorative display, page 54.

Family	
Asteraceae	
Height	
15cm/6in	
Spacing	
25cm/10in <>plants;	
25cm/10in <>rows	
Hardiness	
Tender	
Position	
Full sun; partial shade for summer crops	
Edible parts	
Leaves	
Harvest	
Spring–autumn	

WHERE TO GROW

Lettuce likes light shade in the heat of summer, but for harvests in the cooler seasons grow in a sunny spot. Moisture-retentive soil helps lettuce to produce the best harvests.

HOW TO GROW

Sow from early spring until autumn, depending on cultivar choice. Start the seeds in modules or seed trays, in a temperature of 15°C/59°F; keep the compost moist. When each seedling has four true leaves, harden off and transplant; if you delay after this point in development, the plants may run to seed fairly quickly. Plant with the nursery line just below soil level and water in well. Keep the soil moist while the lettuce establishes. Either harvest lower leaves as required or cut the entire plant once the head has formed. Providing some protection can mean lettuce will crop for most of the year (see Protecting vegetables, page 25).

GROWING TIP

By harvesting the lower leaves of lettuces as the head forms you remove places for slugs to hide.

TYPES OF LETTUCE

Lettuces can be broadly divided into hearting forms or crispheads, and non-hearting varieties, which do not form firm heads and can be grown as cut-and-come-again crops.

Hearting lettuce

Batavian lettuce can be harvested as leaf lettuce; it has thick and crunchy leaves.

Butterhead is a round lettuce, which overwinters well. The leaves have a slightly waxy or buttery texture.

Cos lettuce is tall and has thick leaves. It does well in summer and can be harvested as leaf lettuce.

Iceberg develops a very dense head and needs lots more moisture than other lettuce types.

Non-hearting lettuce

Celtuce/stem lettuce, aka asparagus lettuce, is grown for its thick central stem, but its leaves are also edible.

Leaf types are fantastic for cut-and-come-again salads and form a mass of leaves when mature.

LETTUCE OPIUM

Lettuce produces a milky sap known as lettuce opium from its stems, which in more wild and ancient lettuce strains such as *L. virosa* has sedative and analgesic properties. It is also known as lactucarium and is not as strong in cultivated lettuce.

NOTABLE CULTIVARS

Batavian type
- 'Black Seeded Simpson' is a heritage cultivar.
- 'Mottistone' has red leaves.

Butterhead type
- 'All Year Round', a heritage cultivar from before 1856, will overwinter; has a light green heart.
- 'Marvel of Four Seasons' (aka 'Fat Lazy Blonde') can be overwintered.

Cos type
- 'Little Gem' is reliable and takes around two months to develop a head.
- 'Winter Density' is hardy and produces a small head.

Iceberg type
- 'Webbs Wonderful', a heritage variety from 1890, has delicious, curled, green leaves.

Leaf type
- 'Lollo Rossa' produces dark red leaves.

Cucamelon

Melothria scabra aka Mexican sour gherkin, mouse melon, sandiita

Tiny fruits, which taste like cucumbers with a hint of lime, develop on this vine and add an element of interest to the vegetable garden.

WHERE TO GROW

Grow outdoors in a sunny sheltered spot or in a greenhouse. When planted in moisture-retentive, fertile soil, cucamelons give a fantastic harvest.

HOW TO GROW

Sow in spring, in a minimum temperature of 21°C/70°F. Once germinated, prick out into pots. Harden off before finally planting out once all risk of frost is past. Cucamelons need supports to scramble up (see Natural supports for broad beans, page 128). Keep well watered and feed with a liquid tomato fertilizer during the growing season. Pinch out the growing tip once it reaches the desired height.

GROWING TIP

If winter protection is available, cucamelons can be lifted and treated as perennials, giving them a head start in the second year.

Family	Cucurbitaceae
Height	2.5m/8ft
Spacing	30cm/12in <>plants; 1m/3ft <>rows
Hardiness	Tender
Position	Full sun
Edible parts	Fruits
Harvest	Midsummer–autumn

MALE AND FEMALE
Cucamelons are monoecious, meaning that one plant will produce both male and female flowers so that the plant can pollinate itself.

Watercress
Nasturtium officinale

Stream-dwelling watercress has a peppery flavour and is perfect for the salad bowl. It is a container crop and, as it loves the shade, makes good use of areas where other crops may not thrive.

—

WHERE TO GROW
Watercress may be grown in damp compost, which is sitting in a tray of water, or directly in a container of water in which there is a liquid feed. Outdoors, it needs a shady spot and, being a plant that naturally grows in moving water, moist or wet conditions.

HOW TO GROW
Start from seed or by rooting existing watercress plants (see Rooting watercress, page 94). Sow seed indoors in early spring in a seed tray, but do not cover with compost. Water the compost until it is extremely moist, then place the seed tray in a temperature of 15°C/59°F while the seeds germinate. This should take about two weeks. Once they are large enough, harden off and transplant the seedlings to their final growing positions.

GROWING TIP
If growing directly in water, make sure to change the water regularly before it becomes stagnant, especially in summer.

Family	Brassicaceae
Height	30cm/12in
Spacing	30cm/12in <>plants; 30cm/12in <>rows
Hardiness	Hardy
Position	Shade
Edible parts	Whole plant
Harvest	Summer–autumn

HEALING WATERCRESS
Watercress is believed to have many healing properties throughout the ages, including anti-balding, mental stimulant and aphrodisiac. In fact, the Greek physician Hippocrates referred to watercress as the 'cure of cures'.

Rooting watercress

Watercress is a delicious salad ingredient, adding a peppery hit to the plate. Naturally growing on chalky streams, this leafy crop is a fun and easy crop to grow at home. It can be started from seed, as described on page 93, but another way of cultivating watercress is to propagate it from existing plants, which root easily in water. Rather than buying watercress plants specially, have a go at propagating from the watercress – preferably organic to avoid chemical use – found in a salad bag or bunches from the farmers' market. In order to end up with around six rooted stems, choose around twelve long stems to root in case some do not work; if they do all take, the leaves are still delicious and edible.

Propagate the watercress indoors on a windowsill as it will root more readily in the warmth. The container may be a well-washed jar or a small glass, preferably clear so that the root development can be observed. Using tap water is fine as the plants are used to chalky water in the wild, and most rainwater tends to be on the acidic side. Keep the water level in the jar topped up so that emerging roots do not dry out.

Once roots have fully formed, watercress can be grown on in water or very damp, fertile soil (see page 93). Pick a little as and when needed. Once the plant goes to seed, the taste will get very strong, at which point it is worth propagating more watercress.

1. Select watercress with a long stem, ideally with a small amount of root already protruding from the base.
2. Strip the lower leaves to avoid them sitting in water and rotting. Those at the top are needed for photosynthesis to occur.
3. Fill a jar or small, clear container with fresh water and insert the watercress, with the remaining leaves above the water.
4. Watch carefully for roots to form. This should take around a week. Change the water every few days to avoid build-up of algae.
5. Once the roots are 2.5cm/1in long, transplant to the final growing position.

Oca

Oxalis tuberosa aka cubio, New Zealand yam, uqa

The oca plant has low-growing foliage and pink or yellow edible tubers, which have a distinctive lemony taste.

—

WHERE TO GROW
Needs free-draining soil and full sun. Oca can be grown in a large pot in the greenhouse or polytunnel in areas with a cool climate.

HOW TO GROW
Oca requires a long growing season, so plant its tubers in small pots in a greenhouse in spring. Once there is little risk of frost and the soil has warmed, harden off and plant out into the final position. Keep well watered throughout summer. Harvest once the leaves have died back.

GROWING TIP
There is currently work to breed ocas that produce larger tubers, so keep an eye out for such advances with this vegetable.

Family	Oxalidaceae
Height	30cm/12in
Spacing	90cm/36in <>plants; 90cm/36in <>rows
Hardiness	Tender
Position	Full sun
Edible parts	Tubers, leaves
Harvest	Autumn

SHORT DAYS
Oca is what is known as a short-day plant, meaning that it does not start to form tubers until the days become shorter than the nights. Many other crops such as potatoes started out like this, but have had this quality bred out of them.

Parsnip
Pastinaca sativa

This staple winter crop, which can be stored in the ground for the entire season, needs to be thought about a whole year in advance. Fortunately, these tasty roots are well worth the planning (see also Festive winter vegetables, page 124).

—

WHERE TO GROW
Thrives in light sandy soil and full sun. Create a fine tilth where the parsnips are to be grown, removing the largest stones to avoid forking of the roots.

HOW TO GROW
In mid- to late spring, sow directly into the soil where the parsnips are to grow, in a drill 2cm/¾in deep. Keep the area moist while the seeds are germinating. Water consistently throughout summer.

GROWING TIP
As parsnips are slow to germinate and grow, intersow with radishes (see Succession/Intercropping/Catch cropping, page 24) to mark out the row and provide two crops from the space.

NOTABLE CULTIVARS
- 'Gladiator' is very vigorous and produces a long root.
- 'Tender and True' is reliable and forms medium-sized roots.

Family
Apiaceae
Height
60cm/24in
Spacing
20cm/8in <>plants;
30cm/12in <>rows
Hardiness
Hardy
Position
Full sun
Edible parts
Roots
Harvest
Autumn–early spring

SWEET FREEZE
Frosts will break down the stored starches in parsnips, turning them into sugars and giving a sweeter-flavoured harvest.

Parsley root

Petroselinum crispum var. *tuberosum* aka Hamburg parsley

This variety of parsley develops large, white, edible roots, resembling parsnips. They add a parsley flavour to winter dishes.

—

WHERE TO GROW

Needs free-draining soil covered by a layer of organic matter around 2.5cm/1in deep. Benefits from as much sun as can be afforded but will tolerate light shade.

HOW TO GROW

In early spring sow seeds around 1cm/½in deep directly into the growing area. Then water well. Keep seeds moist until they germinate. Also water this crop consistently throughout summer. Harvest from late summer until late winter, leaving *in situ* until needed.

GROWING TIP

The leaves of parsley root are also edible and can be harvested when the root is pulled.

Family	
Apiaceae	
Height	
30cm/12in	
Spacing	
25cm/10in <>plants;	
25cm/10in <>rows	
Hardiness	
Hardy	
Position	
Full sun	
Edible parts	
Root, leaves	
Harvest	
Late summer–winter	

SUPPENGRÜN

Suppengrün or soup greens are vegetables and herbs in German soups that utilize beef or poultry and include parsley root, leeks, carrots and celery.

Runner bean

Phaseolus coccineus

Runner beans are a fantastic late-summer crop that can be harvested as fresh pods or dried as beans to store over winter.

—

WHERE TO GROW

Needs a hot, sheltered spot and fertile soil. The vines grow to 2m/7ft so ensure sturdy supports can be erected to this height (see also Natural supports for broad beans, page 128).

HOW TO GROW

Sow in pots in late spring or directly into the vegetable garden once there is little risk of frost and temperatures have reached 20°C/68°F. Harden off and plant out once each seedling has one set of true leaves. Tie each stem to a support. Water well and feed with a liquid tomato fertilizer throughout the season.

GROWING TIP

Runner beans like to keep their roots cool so help to maintain moisture by underplanting them with a leafy crop such as lettuce (see page 90) or cucumber (see page 71).

NOTABLE CULTIVARS
- 'Hestia' is a dwarf variety and perfect for a container.
- 'White Lady' has white flowers; its pods are delicious when harvested very small and are not as stringy as other types of runner bean.

Family
Fabaceae
Height
2m/7ft
Spacing
30cm/12in <>plants;
60cm/24in <>rows
Hardiness
Tender
Position
Full sun
Edible parts
Seed pods, seeds
Harvest
Late summer–autumn

NITROGEN FIXATION
Like most legumes, runner beans have nodules on their roots, which help fix nitrogen. In this process, atmospheric nitrogen (which is not accessible to plants) is converted into a useful form with the aid of symbiotic bacteria.

French bean

Phaseolus vulgaris

French beans are a colourful summer crop, in shades from green to yellow to purple (see also Using vegetables as a decorative display, page 54). They are an easy crop to grow, and for those without much space there are plenty of dwarf cultivars to fit in a small area or container.

—

WHERE TO GROW

Needs a sheltered spot to avoid damage to leaves from wind and to encourage pollinators to visit. Give French beans as much sun as possible, ensure the ground is fertile and provide sturdy supports for the climbing varieties (see Natural supports for broad beans, page 128).

HOW TO GROW

Sow once the soil temperature has consistently reached 12°C/54°F, probably late spring. Do not sow before this temperature occurs because seeds will simply sit in the ground and rot. If starting indoors, sow into 9cm/3½in pots at a minimum temperature of 15°C/59°F and water well. When the first true leaves have developed, start hardening off and, once there is little risk of frost, plant into the final growing space. Keep well watered throughout the season and feed every two weeks with a liquid tomato fertilizer. French bean seed can be saved for the following season (see Seed saving, page 118).

GROWING TIP

French beans grow well if their roots are kept moist and cool. The easiest way to achieve this is to underplant with a crop such as lettuce (which likes to be in the shade; see page 90) or a trailing plant such as cucumber (see page 71).

Family
Fabaceae
Height
2m/7ft
Spacing
30cm/12in <>plants;
50cm/20in <>rows
Hardiness
Tender
Position
Full sun
Edible parts
Seed pods, seeds
Harvest
Summer

TAKE A BEAN TO BED
French bean leaves have microscopic hairs on them, which can trap insects. Historically in Balkan countries, bean leaves were strewn on the floors of homes infested with bedbugs, which got caught in the hairs and were then disposed of.

NOTABLE CULTIVARS
- 'Borlotto Lingua Di Fuoco' produces red-speckled pods, which can be eaten young or be dried and stored for winter.
- 'Cobra' produces long, green pods over several weeks.
- 'Kew Blue' has purple pods; it is rumoured to have been developed at the Royal Botanic Gardens, Kew.

Tomatillo

Physalis philadelphica

Tomatillos are encased in paper husks and come in hues from green to yellow to purple (see also Using vegetables as a decorative display, page 54). Plants are high yielding, and their fruits can be frozen or made into chutney for storage. With a taste of tomato and a hint of lime, they also make a tasty salsa.

WHERE TO GROW

Needs a sunny, sheltered position and free-draining soil. Tomatillos can be staked (see Natural supports for broad beans, page 128) or allowed to fall to the ground where, halfway through their growth cycle, they develop rooted lateral growth, which bears more fruits.

HOW TO GROW

Sow in modules in spring and place at 18°C/65°F to germinate. Prick out into pots and allow to grow on until there is little risk of frost. Harden off, plant out into the final growing position and water in well. While flowering, tomatillos will respond well to a liquid tomato feed every two weeks. Tomatillos eventually break through their paper casings but can also be harvested before this, when they are the size of walnuts.

GROWING TIP

Tomatillos need cross-pollination to set fruit, so grow several plants.

Family	Solanaceae
Height	1m/3ft
Spacing	45cm/18in <>plants; 1m/3ft <>rows
Hardiness	Tender
Position	Full sun
Edible parts	Fruits
Harvest	Summer–autumn

AN OLD SOUL
The wild tomatillo is one of the oldest plants to be evidenced in the Solanaceae family, with a fossilized plant being dated to 52 million years ago.

101

Pea

Pisum sativum

One of the vegetables really worth growing at home are peas because they are incredibly sweet when eaten straight off the plant. Being an early-summer treat, this is one of the first new crops to mature.

—

WHERE TO GROW

Needs a sunny spot with organic matter added to the ground because peas are heavy feeders. Support plants with peasticks or netting (see also Natural supports for broad beans, page 128).

HOW TO GROW

Sow in early autumn to overwinter or at the end of winter for a late-spring harvest, when peas crop the best. Sowing in 9cm/3½in pots, hardening off and transplanting into the ground once soil temperature has reached 5°C/41°F is the best course of action, especially for early sowings.

GROWING TIP

Peas can be categorized as early, main-crop and dwarf types. Sowing a mixture will give you a succession of peas in late spring and early summer.

Family	
Fabaceae	
Height	
80cm/32in	
Spacing	
5cm/2in <>plants;	
1m/3ft <>rows	
Hardiness	
Hardy	
Position	
Full sun	
Edible parts	
Seeds, growing tips	
Harvest	
Late spring–early summer	

GREEN GENES
Peas were used in experiments by Gregor Mendel in the mid-nineteenth century, to prove the laws of inheritance in genes.

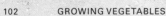

NOTABLE CULTIVARS

- 'Alderman', a heritage main-crop variety introduced in 1891, is high yielding and particularly delicious.
- 'Onward' is a reliable main-crop pea; 'Early Onward' can also be sown to give a crop around two weeks earlier.

PEA SHOOTS

When peas reach their final height, they can be pinched out and the tips eaten, but pea shoots can be grown as a harvest in their own right and this adds diversity to the growing year. They also do well when grown as a windowsill salad (see page 104). When growing pea shoots, use any dried peas as they will not be allowed to grow tall or flower, so be sure to check the cultivar information.

Outdoors, once the soil warms to 5°C/41°F, plant pea seed thickly and around 5cm/2in deep. In areas where pigeons are a problem, netting may be needed to protect this crop. Sow in succession for a crop all the way through to winter if desired. Once pea shoots reach around 15cm/6in tall, harvest up to 10cm/4in of the top growth, preferably snipping off just above a node. This shoot will regrow, giving at least another harvest. The shoots will eventually become a little tougher or run to flower, which is a good time to do another sowing.

On an indoor windowsill, pea shoots can be cultivated throughout the year, giving a fresh addition to salads even in the coldest months. Fill a container with multipurpose compost and sow thickly and at least 5cm/2in deep. Keep watered throughout the growing process. Harvest as for outdoor-grown pea shoots.

Windowsill salads

Where outdoor space is limited, some crops can be grown indoors. When given light, warmth, water and food, most vegetables will grow and can be harvested as baby plants. Growing indoors on a windowsill will also provide a harvest in the colder months. Two of the easiest crops to grow are cut-and-come-again salads and microgreens.

Microgreens are simply sprouted seeds, which can be scattered over a salad and give an intense hit of flavour. Often harvestable after a week, they are an easy and rewarding crop to attempt. Once the leaves are showing, they are ready for harvest, but they will not re-sprout, so this is the point to sow again, which can be done in the same compost. Many vegetables and herbs are suitable as microgreens including mustards, rocket, spinach, lettuce, basil, coriander and kale.

Cut-and-come-again crops give tender baby leaves for the salad bowl, and the plants will continue growing, giving several harvests from one sowing. Cutting the largest leaves from the plants and leaving the smaller leaves to emerge will give a constant supply, and it may even be worth having several pots growing in succession if salads are a popular harvest. Crops that work as cut-and-come-again include lettuce, mustards, parsley, sorrel, pea shoots and beetroot; special seed mixes can be obtained.

1. Fill the pot with compost, tamping it down to settle the soil level. Smooth the top to give a level surface.
2. Sow seeds fairly thickly over the compost, ensuring even coverage.
3. Cover with a thin layer of compost and water. Place the pot on to a drip tray or saucer to allow for watering and place into a warm, light position such as a windowsill.
4. Harvest when leaves are 10–15cm/4–6in long, by snipping off just above the base of the leaf.
5. Provide a liquid feed after harvesting and allow remaining leaves to continue growing. Each sowing should provide around three harvests.

Mangetout and sugarsnap pea

Pisum sativum

Although requiring the same cultivation, these two types of *Pisum sativum* are different in their stage of harvest: mangetout have tiny peas with the focus on the pod itself whereas sugarsnap peas have large peas when picked.

—

WHERE TO GROW

Need a sunny, sheltered spot and free-draining soil with added organic matter for moisture retention if the soil is particularly sandy. Provide supports for tall cultivars (see Natural supports for broad beans, page 128).

HOW TO GROW

In late winter, start an early crop by sowing in 9cm/3½in pots in the greenhouse. Then, from spring until midsummer, sow directly into the garden soil. Peas need supports to climb up, with netting or peasticks being perfect for them to wrap their tendrils around (see Natural supports for broad beans, page 128). Water well throughout the growing season.

GROWING TIP

Continuous picking of the pods will encourage new flowers to develop, giving a steady harvest for several weeks.

Family
Fabaceae
Height
Up to 2.5m/8ft
Spacing
5cm/2in <>plants;
1.5m/5ft <>rows
Hardiness
Hardy
Position
Full sun
Edible parts
Seed pods, seeds
Harvest
Summer

NOTABLE CULTIVARS

Mangetout
- 'Shiraz' bears dark purple pods.

Sugarsnap pea
- 'Spring Blush' has purple flowers producing two-toned pods.

EAT ALL
Mangetout is French for 'eat all' and refers to eating the peas and the pods of this vegetable. Garden peas have a layer of inedible lignin in their pod walls, which is missing in mangetout so its whole pod can be consumed.

Radish

Raphanus sativus

Radishes are an easy vegetable to grow and are a fantastic plant to use as a catch crop (see Succession/Intercropping/Catch cropping, page 24). They can be grown for most of the year and, along with the edible root, the leaves are delicious, too.

—

WHERE TO GROW
Grows best in fertile, moisture-retentive soil and full sun but tolerates light shade.

HOW TO GROW
Sow directly into the ground in a drill around 1cm/½in deep. Keep well watered throughout the growing period, and bear in mind that the more mature radishes get, the hotter the taste is. Summer radishes take around six weeks to mature, and winter radishes around nine weeks. This is a great crop to sow continuously to always have something to harvest.

GROWING TIP
To get the best from radishes, sow the correct cultivar at the right time. Summer radishes are small, rounded, cylindrical or pointed, whereas winter ones are larger and resemble turnips.

Family	
Brassicaceae	
Height	
20cm/8in	
Spacing	
5cm/2in <>plants;	
30cm/12in <>rows	
Hardiness	
Hardy	
Position	
Full sun	
Edible parts	
Root, leaves	
Harvest	
Spring–early winter	

A TRUE COMPANION
Radishes make a fantastic companion crop as their strong smell can deter aphids and other insects (see Pests, page 132–4). They can also be sacrificial plants for other brassicas suffering from flea beetles, which live in the soil. If such larger brassicas are underplanted with radishes, the beetle will eat the radishes first, but it does not damage the roots so the radishes are still edible.

NOTABLE CULTIVARS
- 'Black Spanish Round' is a dark-skinned, heritage winter variety.
- 'Cherry Belle' is fast growing, with a rounded shape.
- 'French Breakfast' is a long, red-and-white summer cultivar from around 1865.

Radish pod

Raphanus sativus

All radishes form edible seed pods, but some are specifically cultivated for this trait. Such pods make a spicy snack when eaten raw or lightly cooked.

—

WHERE TO GROW
Prefers fertile, moisture-retentive soil and full sun but tolerates light shade.

HOW TO GROW
In spring and early summer, sow outdoors in drills around 1cm/½in deep, and thin to 15cm/6in apart once germinated. Plants quickly run to flower then develop bean-like pods, which will be harvestable around six weeks after sowing. Harvest them when young and green. Pods of some cultivars can grow to over 30cm/12in long.

GROWING TIP
Sow several plants every few weeks for a continuous supply from spring to autumn.

Family
Brassicaceae
Height
30cm/12in
Spacing
15cm/6in <>plants;
30cm/12in <>rows
Hardiness
Hardy
Position
Full sun
Edible parts
Seed pods, root
Harvest
Late spring–autumn

SPICY SNACK
Radish pods are traditionally sliced thinly and salted in Germany, and then served with bread and butter.

NOTABLE CULTIVARS
• 'München Bier' produces both edible white roots and delicious pods, which are around 10cm/4in long.
• 'Rat's Tail' bears large, spicy pods.

Rhubarb

Rheum × hybridum

Rhubarb is a perennial crop with dark pink, edible stems. Although mainly eaten as a fruit in sweet dishes, it is, in fact, a vegetable and adds interest to savoury courses.

—

WHERE TO GROW

Needs as much sun as possible and free-draining soil. Rhubarb can also be grown successfully in a large pot.

HOW TO GROW

Plant rhubarb crowns in autumn or spring into ground with plenty of additional manure. Ensure the top of the crown is above the soil level, water well and surround each crown with a doughnut of mulch. Allow rhubarb to grow for a full season before harvesting, so the plant can establish. In its second spring, harvest by pulling the stems from the base of the plant in early spring. Mulch annually in autumn as rhubarb is a heavy feeder.

GROWING TIP

Although rhubarb can be harvested from spring to autumn if only a little is taken each time, it is invaluable in early spring. If harvesting plenty at this time of year, stop cropping around early summer, to allow the plant to store energy for next year's harvest.

Family
Polygonaceae
Height
75cm/30in
Spacing
75cm/30in <>plants;
75cm/30in <>rows
Hardiness
Hardy
Position
Full sun
Edible parts
Stems
Harvest
Spring–early summer

THE TUSKY TRIANGLE
The Tusky or Rhubarb Triangle is an area in West Yorkshire in the UK renowned for its forced rhubarb – tusky being a Yorkshire term for rhubarb. The crop is forced by growing it in warm, completely dark conditions (see Forced rhubarb, page 110). As the plant cannot photosynthesize, it forces the rhubarb to use reserved supplies of carbohydrate to grow stems to search for the light. The carbohydrate is turned into glucose in this process, producing sweet and tender rhubarb stems.

NOTABLE CULTIVARS
- 'Champagne' is an early cultivar, with pink stems.
- 'Victoria' is reliable; named after Queen Victoria.

Forced rhubarb

Forced vegetables have undergone a process whereby light is removed, so that the plant uses its reserves of carbohydrate to promote growth while it searches for light. This carbohydrate turns into sugar, creating sweet and tender stems. Forcing takes place in late winter and early spring as plants come into growth, and the resulting crops are a delicacy, highly priced in supermarkets. Such stems are much paler than their forced counterparts. When forced, the harvest can be up to a month earlier than usual. The earliest crops can be obtained with heat from the addition of materials such as manure or by growing crowns in pots to force indoors.

Several vegetable plants can be forced, including rhubarb, seakale and chicory. This can be done *in situ* or the crown or root can be dug up and taken indoors (see Chicory, page 68). These plants are placed in a little compost and their roots kept moist. Light is then removed and the forcing process undertaken, as for those forced outdoors. Ensure plants being taken indoors have experienced some cold, as many perennial vegetables need this to break dormancy.

Once plants have been forced, they can be replanted, but do not harvest them for the rest of the year to allow them to regain strength. Keep track of which plants were forced and avoid using these crowns in successive years. Plants that have been forced will benefit from feeding once the crop has been harvested.

Little equipment is needed for forcing in the domestic garden, although specific forcing pots are available. However, any pot or bucket that does not taper can be utilized, provided it is frostproof (at this time of year there can be cold spells) and tall enough to allow the forced stems to grow to a decent height around 60cm/24in.

1. Once buds are showing on the rhubarb, or the stems have just come into growth, begin the forcing process.
2. Cover each crown with a large, frost-proof pot, ensuring complete darkness. If the pot has drainage holes, cover them. Press the lip of the pot firmly into the ground.
3. If available, cover the pot with manure, straw, fleece or compost to increase the heat within the forcing pot.
4. Depending on the weather, the forcing process can take 2–4 weeks. Once the leaves touch the top of the pot, the crop is ready to harvest.
5. Pick the forced rhubarb stems by giving a sharp sideways tug to the base of each stem.

Buckler-leaf sorrel

Rumex scutatus aka French sorrel

There are several different sorrels that can be harvested for the plate – all adding a different character. One of them is buckler-leaf sorrel, a perennial with an unusual leaf shape and a delicious citrus flavour.

—

WHERE TO GROW

Grows in full sun or partial shade and needs moisture-retentive soil. This is a perennial plant, which should last for ten years, so do not plant in a rotational bed.

HOW TO GROW

In spring or autumn, sow in seed trays under glass and prick out once plants are large enough. When the roots have filled out their pot, move into the final position, water in well and mulch around each plant. Harvest young leaves regularly throughout the year.

GROWING TIP

Although buckler-leaf sorrel will grow through a drought, its leaves will become tough. If this happens, cut back and give the new growth lots of care and water.

Family	
Polygonaceae	
Height	
20cm/8in	
Spacing	
60cm/24in <>plants;	
60cm/24in <>rows	
Hardiness	
Hardy	
Position	
Full sun or partial shade	
Edible parts	
Leaves	
Harvest	
Spring–autumn	

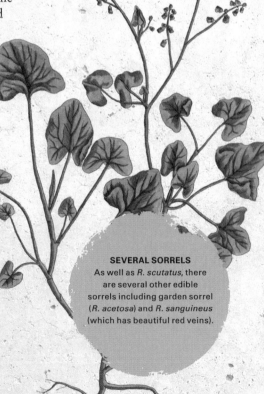

SEVERAL SORRELS
As well as *R. scutatus*, there are several other edible sorrels including garden sorrel (*R. acetosa*) and *R. sanguineus* (which has beautiful red veins).

Agretti

Salsola soda

Agretti is a fleshy leaf crop similar to marsh samphire (*Salicornia bigelovii*) except that it grows on land. It can be eaten raw or cooked.

WHERE TO GROW

Needs full sun. Being a coastal plant, agretti prefers free-draining soil; add plenty of organic matter to this.

HOW TO GROW

In late winter, soak seeds for twenty-four hours to improve germination. Then sow in a seed tray and place it under glass at a temperature of 18°C/65°F. Within twenty-one days there should be germination. Prick out and allow the seedlings to grow on until mid-spring. Then harden off and plant out into the prepared rich soil. Harvest little and often.

GROWING TIP

Agretti seed has a short viability window; therefore, sow seed as soon as possible after purchase. Delayed sowing or seed saved for too long is unlikely to germinate.

Family	
Amaranthaceae	
Height	
20cm/8in	
Spacing	
15cm/6in <>plants;	
30cm/12in <>rows	
Hardiness	
Hardy	
Position	
Full sun	
Edible parts	
Leaves	
Harvest	
Summer–autumn	

GREEN GLASS
Historically, agretti was burnt to make soda ash, which was used as an alkali in soap and glassmaking.

Yacon

Smallanthus sonchifolius aka Peruvian ground apple

A relative of the sunflower (*Helianthus*), yacon is
originally from the Andes. Its edible tubers have
a refreshing apple taste in autumn.

—

WHERE TO GROW
Needs a sunny, sheltered spot and free-draining
soil, with added organic matter to help retain
moisture. Yacon grows well in a greenhouse,
where it will have a longer season to mature.

HOW TO GROW
In mid-spring, plant tubers in pots indoors in
frost-prone areas. Once the soil has warmed to
at least 7°C/45°C and there is little risk of frost,
harden off and plant out. Water in well and
mulch around each plant, to retain moisture.
When the leaves die back in autumn, dig up the
tubers. Store the smallest ones in a cool, dark,
frost-free area over winter for use the next year.
In milder areas, yacon can overwinter *in situ*.

GROWING TIP
If it is not possible to grow yacon in a sheltered
spot, stake each plant, to avoid stems snapping in
the wind.

Family
Asteraceae
Height
1.5m/5ft
Spacing
50cm/20in <>plants;
1m/3ft <>rows
Hardiness
Tender
Position
Full sun
Edible parts
Tubers
Harvest
Autumn

SWEET SUBSTITUTION
Yacon tubers contain
fructooligosaccharides,
which taste sweet but are not
metabolized by humans. The
tubers are now being turned
into a syrup that is a low-calorie
replacement for sugar.

Tomato

Solanum lycopersicum

A fresh tomato is one of the joys of summer from the vegetable garden. This crop comes in a large array of colours, sizes, shapes and flavours, plus with various growth habits, so everyone can find room for a tomato plant (see also Using vegetables as a decorative display, page 54). It is possible to grow tomatoes from seed that you have saved yourself (see Seed saving, page 118).

—

WHERE TO GROW

Although traditionally this crop has been cultivated under glass in frost-prone regions, to give tomatoes the temperatures needed, new cultivars have since been bred to grow well outdoors. There, they will ripen slightly later than those under glass, and so the season can be extended. Tomatoes need a sunny, sheltered site and are very heavy feeders so the addition of organic matter to the soil is essential.

Family
Solanaceae
Height
2m/7ft
Spacing
50cm/20in <>plants;
50cm/20in <>rows
Hardiness
Tender
Position
Full sun, sheltered
Edible parts
Fruits
Harvest
Summer–autumn

WHAT IS THE BUZZ?
The flowers on tomatoes are buzz pollinated, meaning that they release pollen only when a flower is shaken by the buzzing of a bee, causing the anthers to drop pollen directly on to the bee's body.

HOW TO GROW

Sow in seed trays in spring, and leave in a temperature of
21°C/70°F during germination, pricking out into modules
once they have their first true leaves. Pot up plants into
9cm/3½in pots and continue to grow them at the same
heat level. Slowly harden them off before planting out once
there is little risk of frost.

Alternatively, buy tomatoes as plants with grafted
rootstocks, where the rootstock provides disease
resistance to blight and viruses, for example (see Diseases,
page 134), and gives higher yields than more disease-
susceptible cultivars.

Support tomatoes in their final planting positions; this
could be by suspended strings in a greenhouse, or by
sturdy canes outdoors (see Natural supports for broad
beans, page 128). Water consistently and feed using a liquid
tomato fertilizer weekly. Pinch out side shoots on cordon
varieties. Remove the leader on each plant at the end of
summer, or once the plant fills its growing space. At this
point, do not allow the plant to produce any new fruits,
and thin out younger fruits to allow the plant to put all its
energies into ripening existing fruits.

GROWING TIP

When watering tomatoes, apply water directly to the roots,
avoiding leaf areas. This not only helps to deter the spread of
blight (see page 134), but also avoids watermarks on the fruits
and leaves.

TYPES OF TOMATO GROWTH HABIT

Tomatoes have several different growth habits, each requiring a different cultivation technique.

Bush or determinate plants are a newer introduction as the gene for this growth habit did not appear until the 1920s. This gene means that the plant reaches a final height and flowers in clusters at the end of branches. Bush tomatoes do not need side shoots removed, nor any supports. Harvesting can take slightly longer than on a cordon tomato plant because the fruits are hidden.

Cordon or indeterminate tomatoes are the most commonly grown and they need support. They have a large central stem with lateral trusses on which they produce fruits. From the points where these trusses meet the main stem, cordon tomatoes also grow secondary side shoots, usually at a slight upwards angle from the truss. These side shoots will start to behave like stems, producing fruit trusses and more side shoots, which exhausts the plants. For this reason, side shoots are removed as soon as they appear.

Dwarf and trailing tomatoes make perfect plants for a hanging basket or a kitchen windowsill.

NOTABLE CULTIVARS

Bush
- 'Sub-Arctic Plenty' grows well in cool-temperature areas.

Cordon
- 'Outdoor Girl' is heavy cropping and produces well when grown outdoors.
- 'Sungold' produces a good crop of orange cherry fruits.

Trailing
- 'Tumbler' is good for a hanging basket.

The colour of a tomato is dictated by a combination of the flesh colour and the skin colour:

- Brown = yellow skin and red/green flesh
- Pink = clear skin and red flesh
- Purple = clear skin and red/green flesh (flesh has a recessive gene which retains some chlorophyll once ripe)
- Red = yellow skin and red flesh
- White = clear skin and white flesh
- Yellow = clear skin and yellow flesh.

Seed saving

Saving seed is an interesting and rewarding aspect of vegetable gardening, and in most circumstances is incredibly easy. Before saving, it is useful to find out whether the seed will come true, which means the seed saved will grow into the same cultivar as its parent. If plants are cross-pollinated, they may contain genetic information from two cultivars, creating different characteristics, although this is how breeding occurs and can lead to some interesting results. If the seed does not come true, isolation distances can be imposed, or barriers erected to stop insects cross-pollinating parent plants. Tomatoes mainly come true from seed, but, to guarantee this, grow six plants of the same cultivar at least 3m/10ft away from any other cultivars. Although it is still worth researching, cultivars such as 'Ailsa Craig' reliably come true.

Seeds need to be fully ripe before harvesting. In the case of legumes (see French bean, page 100, or Pea, page 102), they can be left to completely dry on the plant. Biennials such as carrots, parsnips and kale require a period of cold to induce flowering and seed production; often this means leaving them in the ground over winter and collecting the seed in spring, but if the plant is not hardy, or a cold winter is expected, lift the crop and replant indoors. If it is not possible for seeds to dry on the plant, bring in their pods and pop them into a container or bag, and label it clearly.

Before storing seeds, remove as much plant debris as possible – by hand, sieving or winnowing in the case of dried plants. Some seeds are contained within a gel or other wet material, in which case fermentation of this wet material should be induced to remove it. Once seeds are cleaned, store in a cool, dry room in a fully labelled paper envelope in a cool, dark container until ready to be used.

1. Harvest the tomatoes when fully ripe, choosing ones with no disease and which look true to type by comparing them to images of the expected fruits.
2. Scoop out the seeds and surrounding gel. Place in a jar of water, cover with a lid which has holes, and leave in an area of 25°C/77°F for 3–5 days, to allow the gel to ferment.
3. Scoop off the mould and gel mixture, which will have floated to the top, and wash the remaining seeds with fresh water.
4. Sieve the clean seeds and place them on to a coffee filter to dry out thoroughly.
5. Put the dried seeds into a labelled envelope and store in a cool, dark place over winter.

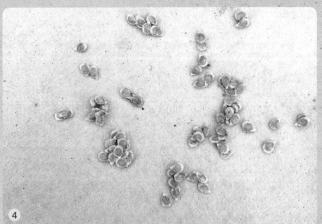

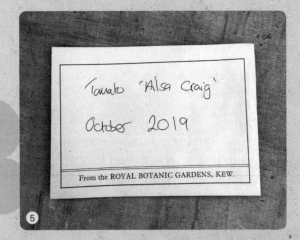

Tomato 'Ailsa Craig'
October 2019

From the ROYAL BOTANIC GARDENS, KEW.

Aubergine

Solanum melongena aka eggplant

Aubergines come in different shapes and are best harvested when small but fully coloured. Although usually dark purple, there are white and orange cultivars, too. See also Using vegetables as a decorative display, page 54.

—

WHERE TO GROW

Typically a greenhouse crop in cool areas, to give them the heat and humidity required for growth, aubergines will also do well outdoors in a hot summer if given a sunny, sheltered situation and free-draining soil.

HOW TO GROW

In early spring, germinate seed under glass, providing a minimum temperature of 21°C/70°F. Prick out seedlings into modules and eventually plant in 9cm/3½in pots once the roots have filled the modules. Let the plants fill the pot and harden off before planting out once there is little risk of frost. Provide supports for aubergines (see Natural supports for broad beans, page 128) and keep well watered throughout summer. Harvest when small.

GROWING TIP

Encouraging a bushy habit by pinching out the growing tip will increase fruit production, although fruits will need thinning if you aim for larger ones.

Family
Solanaceae
Height
50cm/20in
Spacing
60cm/24in <>plants;
80cm/32in <>rows
Hardiness
Tender
Position
Full sun
Edible parts
Fruits
Harvest
Summer–autumn

NOTABLE CULTIVARS
- 'Black Enorma' is compact and grows well in a pot; has less spiny stems than other cultivars.
- 'Turkish Orange' has rounded, orange fruit, slightly resembling tomatoes.

THE MAD APPLE
Solanum melongena goes by many names including aubergine and egg plant, but it was also historically known as the mad apple and in some folklore was thought to cause insanity.

Potato

Solanum tuberosum

One of the staple crops in the vegetable garden is potatoes, which are classified by the length of time they take to mature: first earlies, second earlies and main-crop. Although potatoes will continue to grow past their optimum harvesting point, their characteristic flavours are lost if left in the ground for too long: for example, a waxy 'Jersey Royal' will stay in the ground until the end of summer, growing bigger but will take on a floury texture.

—

Family	
Solanaceae	
Height	
60cm/24in	
Spacing	
60cm/24in <>plants;	
75cm/30in <>rows	
Hardiness	
Tender	
Position	
Full sun	
Edible parts	
Tubers	
Harvest	
Summer–autumn	

WHERE TO GROW
Needs full sun and fertile soil in which plenty of organic matter has been added before planting, because potatoes are heavy feeders.

HOW TO GROW
Plant seed potatoes 15cm/6in deep in long drills in mid-spring. Potatoes are not hardy, so if shoots appear above ground when a frost is forecast cover them with soil from between the rows – a process known as earthing up. Ensure the soil is kept consistently watered during the growing season, to avoid the appearance of scab on the skins. After harvesting, potatoes are best eaten immediately or stored in a root clamp (see page 80). See also Types of potato, page 123.

GROWING TIP
Before planting your seed potatoes, they can be chitted on a windowsill or in a frost-free greenhouse to encourage growth of stems, giving a head start on the planting season.

NOTABLE CULTIVARS

First earlies

- 'Foremost' is a reliable, waxy potato with white flesh.
- 'International Kidney' (aka Jersey Royals – technically called Jersey Royals only when grown in Jersey, where they are given lots of seaweed) has a waxy flavour.

Second earlies

- 'Charlotte' is a reliable salad potato with a pale skin and creamy flesh.
- 'Ratte', a French heritage variety, has a waxy yellow flesh with a slightly nutty flavour.

Main-crop

- 'King Edward', one of the best-known baking potatoes, is high yielding and has pink patches on the skin.
- 'Pink Fir Apple' has a slightly pink skin and yellow flesh; this heritage potato was first introduced in 1850.

DIG FOR VICTORY

Potatoes have long been grown at the Royal Botanic Gardens, Kew, and in 1918 the Palace Lawn was ploughed to plant potatoes, and 27 tonnes were harvested that August to help the war effort. During the Second World War, the curator of the gardens, William Campbell, discovered that potatoes could be cultivated from slices as long as they contained an 'eye', which meant the dwindling stock of seed potatoes went farther.

TYPES OF POTATO

First earlies are the first potatoes out of the ground and one of the signs that the harvest season has begun. They are ready 10–12 weeks after planting, once the plants start to flower and are delicious as salad potatoes. They have a waxy flesh and thin skin, making them perfect for boiling and roasting, but they do not store well, so enjoy them while they last.

Second earlies are ready to harvest 13–16 weeks after planting. They have both waxy and floury characteristics. Harvest once the foliage starts to turn yellow and die back.

Main-crop potatoes take around twenty-four weeks to mature and give large tubers with thick skins, which are perfect for storing and eating at festive occasions (see Festive winter vegetables, page 124). Wait until the foliage has fully died back and then leave in the soil for a further two weeks if the weather is forecast to remain dry.

Festive winter vegetables

Looking down at a festive dinner plate and realizing that most of the vegetables have been harvested from your plot is a rewarding and joyful experience. It is entirely possible to achieve this with a little planning.

Roast potatoes are fantastic and, if the grower can offer a little protection, potatoes can be harvested in mid-winter. They will need at least twelve weeks to be ready so, in mid- to late summer, buy cultivars such as 'Red Duke of York' or 'Maris Piper' directly from the supplier as the tubers need a period of cold to be able to break dormancy. Plant in a greenhouse and on the day of the meal pull them up, remove the haulms and cook. If no winter protection is available, summer crops can be stored until mid-winter, to be eaten when required.

Alongside the potatoes, sow quick-maturing varieties of small carrots. Early autumn-sown beetroot for roasting can also be grown in a greenhouse, with the tops adding tasty greens to the festive plate.

Parsnips and swedes will still be growing in the ground and be simply harvested as and when required. From the brassica family, Brussels sprouts, kale and savoy cabbage can be taken from the plot. Leeks will be standing tall in the vegetable garden, although in extremely cold winters some protection should be provided. From the dry store, onions and garlic give a hit of summer, and squash can be chosen and roasted.

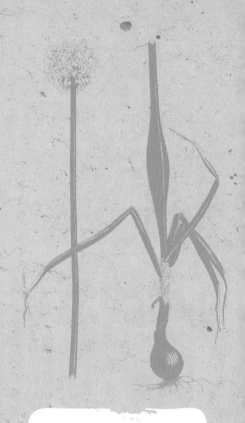

A Potatoes: fill a growing bag or large container with multipurpose compost until about half full, place in 1–3 tubers then cover with compost, leaving room to earth up.

B Parsnips: even when started in late spring, this crop will still happily stay in the ground in early winter; simply pull up as required.

C Kale (started in midsummer) and Brussels sprouts (started in late spring) will still be growing on the plot, so harvest as required.

D Carrots: choose a small type such as Paris Market and plant in multipurpose compost in early autumn. Keep well watered and thin as needed.

E Garlic and onions: dry in summer and store for use in the festive period.

Spinach

Spinacia oleracea

Spinach produces dark green leaves that can be cropped throughout the year. Known for its iron content, spinach is delicious as a baby leaf, raw in salad or cooked in winter dishes.

—

WHERE TO GROW

Grow especially summer crops in partial shade. Spinach enjoys moisture-retentive soil with plenty of additional organic matter. It is also suitable as a windowsill salad (see page 104).

HOW TO GROW

Sow in succession, either directly in the ground, or in modules under glass. Winter and spring sowings are best started indoors, hardened off and transplanted once seedlings are large enough to handle, then watered well. Keep well watered to avoid bolting. Harvest by removing a few lower leaves from each plant at a time.

GROWING TIP

If overwintering spinach, ensure the seed is sown by late summer, to allow the plants to get large enough throughout autumn to survive winter.

NOTABLE CULTIVARS
- 'Atlanta' is an invaluable overwintering variety.
- 'Red Kitten' has red stems.

Family	Amaranthaceae
Height	30cm/12in
Spacing	15cm/6in <>plants; 30cm/12in <>rows
Hardiness	Hardy
Position	Partial shade
Edible parts	Leaves
Harvest	Year-round

A QUEEN'S GREENS
Dishes that contain spinach often contain the word 'Florentine' in their title. This is because Queen Catherine de' Medici, born in Florence, loved spinach so much that it was served for every meal.

Lamb's lettuce

Valerianella locusta aka corn salad

This vegetable is a fantastic winter salad ingredient – its rosettes providing dark green leaves throughout the cold months when there is little else growing.

—

WHERE TO GROW
Needs full sun and free-draining, fertile soil so add organic matter.

HOW TO GROW
Sow *in situ* except for a winter crop, which is sown in modules in late summer. Harden off and transplant into the vegetable garden as soon as the seedlings are large enough, watering in well and mulching around each plant. Harvest leaves as required.

GROWING TIP
If overwintering lamb's lettuce, giving some protection will produce a better harvest (see Protecting vegetables, page 25).

Family	
Caprifoliaceae	
Height	
10cm/4in	
Spacing	
10cm/4in <>plants;	
15cm/6in <>rows	
Hardiness	
Hardy	
Position	
Full sun	
Edible parts	
Leaves	
Harvest	
Year-round	

A FAIRYTALE HARVEST
In the original story of Rapunzel, the child was named after the green salad leaves that her mother was craving while pregnant. Rapunzel is a German name for *Valerianella locusta.*

Natural supports for broad beans

Vegetable cultivars are bred for the quality of
the harvest and often disease resistance, which
sometimes means their ability to support
themselves has been reduced. Thus, many crops
require extra support from the vegetable gardener,
especially tall plants on an open site. Plants that
would naturally climb in the wild will need
something to scramble up, and others will require
a helping hand to stop them falling over once
laden with fruits. Crops needing supports to climb
up include beans and peas, while others such as
cucumbers, which are scrambling plants, will
benefit from being raised away from the ground
so that fruit does not get damp and rot off, plus
picking can be easier. Crops such as aubergine,
chilli peppers and broad beans will appreciate a
support to stop them bending or falling over once
they start cropping.

Supports are always best put into place while
plants are young and, with these types of crop, can
be individual supports or cages around a group
of plants. The grower has many different options
for the support material, but it must be strong,
tall enough once sunk into the ground and be able
to withstand at least one growing season. Metal
supports are long-lasting and attractive, but often
expensive and quite permanent, which may not be
suitable where crops are rotated. Plastic is cheaper
and easier but does not last very long.

Natural supports are robust, attractive and
sustainable. Woods such as hazel and birch are
often utilized in the vegetable garden. Peasticks
are made from the top of coppiced hazel, and bean
poles from the lower limbs. Growers can also plant
hazel for coppicing, producing their own supports.
This project describes using hazel to create a cage
around broad beans.

1. Plan out the area around the
   broad beans, and measure regular
   intervals to place sturdy hazel
   poles, ensuring middle plants can
   be accessed for harvesting.
2. Saw the bottom of each hazel
   pole to a slope, or whittle it to a
   point, to make it easier to get into
   the ground.
3. Start the hole for each pole with
   a dibber.
4. Insert the bottom of the pole and
   hammer until at least 20cm/8in
   of a 1m/3ft pole is underground.
   Use a spirit level for accuracy,
   to ensure the pole is vertical.
   Beside one of these poles, place a
   peastick made from hazel, starting
   its hole with a dibber. Push into
   the ground.
5. Insert the remaining peasticks
   so that the branches overlap
   as far as the final pole, and
   weave these together to create a
   secure support.

Broad bean

Vicia faba

Hardy broad beans can be planted in autumn to give a welcome early harvest, followed by cultivars sown in late winter. Broad beans are generally light green, but there are pink cultivars available including 'Karmazyn'.

WHERE TO GROW

Needs well-drained soil, especially if overwintering. A sunny spot will encourage the best harvest.

HOW TO GROW

In early autumn, sow overwintering cultivars in 9cm/3½in pots, then harden off and transplant when there is free ground. They need to be planted out by late autumn in order to be established enough to tolerate the cold period. Otherwise sow seeds in late winter, either into 9cm/3½in pots or directly into the soil if it has warmed to 5°C/41°F. Some support may be necessary once plants start to get taller (see Natural supports for broad beans, page 128).

GROWING TIP

Once they start flowering, you can pinch out the tips of broad bean plants as this lush growth attracts black bean aphid (see Aphids, page 132). Add the tips to salads rather than putting them on the compost heap.

Family	
Fabaceae	
Height	
1m/3ft	
Spacing	
25cm/10in <>plants;	
45cm/18in <>rows	
Hardiness	
Hardy	
Position	
Full sun	
Edible parts	
Seeds	
Harvest	
Late spring–early summer	

NOTABLE CULTIVARS

- 'Aquadulce Claudia' is the most reliable long pod for overwintering.
- 'Crimson Flowered' is an extremely old cultivar, from 1777, with beautiful red flowers.
- 'Karmazyn' produces pale pink beans.
- 'The Sutton' has a dwarf habit.

BEAN COUNTERS

In the Netherlands, roasted broad beans are a special treat, called *molleboon*, and until the late eighteenth century were used in the voting process.

Sweetcorn

Zea mays

Sweetcorn is one of the vegetables that tastes so much better when eaten straight off the plant. The cobs comes in a variety of sizes and colours, including rainbow varieties (see also Using vegetables as a decorative display, page 54).

—

WHERE TO GROW
Needs a sunny, sheltered site, and fertile soil. Sweetcorn is best block planted so that when the wind carries the male pollen it is more likely to find a female tassel to pollinate.

HOW TO GROW
In spring, sow in 9cm/3½in pots or modules that give room for long roots and leave in a greenhouse at a temperature of 21°C/70°F for optimum germination. Harden off and plant out once there is little risk of frost. Alternatively, in early summer sow directly outdoors, where pre-warming the soil will help successful germination. Once the plants begins flowering, ensure the soil is kept moist.

GROWING TIP
Sweetcorn is ready for harvesting once the tassels turn brown and the kernel liquid appears milky when squeezed. Harvest as soon as possible for the best flavour.

Family	
Poaceae	
Height	
1.5m/5ft	
Spacing	
45cm/18in <>plants;	
45cm/18in <>rows	
Hardiness	
Tender	
Position	
Full sun	
Edible parts	
Seeds	
Harvest	
Summer–autumn	

SWEET SORROW
Sweetcorn is renowned for tasting much sweeter when eaten straight off the plant. This is because the stored sugars are utilized during post-harvest respiration and transformed into starch.

NOTABLE CULTIVARS
- 'Minipop' F1 produces baby cobs.
- 'Swift' F1 matures earlier than most and has very sweet cobs.

Troubleshooting

Vegetable growing is extremely rewarding, but along the way the grower may encounter a few problems which need to be dealt with. These usually fall under one of three classifications; pests, diseases or disorders. With each individual crop, there are a number of specific problems, but covered here are some of the most common ones and how to manage them.

The easiest way to prevent most problems is to cultivate strong and healthy plants, because they will be able to fight off and survive attacks. Healthy plants are not necessarily the most cosseted ones, but those that have been hardened off well (see Hardening off, page 23), are used to managing the elements from a young age and have produced a strong root structure. They still need human intervention to provide the correct water, nutrients, light and warmth to grow as healthily as possible. If a pest or disease is persistent, the grower can seek out resistant varieties, or it may be worth not growing that crop for several years. Crop rotation also helps to reduce build-up of pests and diseases, as can learning the life cycles of the pests and diseases, and planting to avoid peak times of disease spread and pest reproduction.

PESTS

Pests are creatures that want to eat the crops in a vegetable garden. Although frustrating, if a diverse ecosystem is created attacks from pests will often be short-lived because natural predators will manage the pest population.

Aphids
These sap-sucking insects are one of the most common pests. They mainly attack young, lush-growing tips such as on broad beans (see page 130) and can cause distorted growth. Aphids also secrete a sticky substance called honeydew, which causes secondary infections from the formation of sooty mould. Small attacks of aphids are easily removed by hand, and there are many insects that eat aphids, such as ladybirds, some wasps and hoverfly larvae, so attract these with companion flowers (see Companion planting, page 25). Alternatively, a horticultural soap wash can be sprayed, which effects the cellular membranes of the aphids, stopping this rapidly multiplying pest.

Birds
Crops, especially the leaves of brassicas, legumes and salads, are often attacked by birds. This can stunt growth or remove the entire harvestable crop. Putting up netting as a barrier (see Protecting vegetables, page 25) or using bird scarers often minimizes the damage caused. There is also some evidence that growing red cultivars and mixing up crops in a polyculture can stop birds damaging entire crops.

OPPOSITE Cabbage collars should be at least 10cm/4in in diameter and laid flush with the ground, to stop root flies laying their eggs.

Caterpillars

Caterpillars can cause severe damage to crops, especially to crops such as cabbages (see page 57), which the cabbage white butterfly likes to lay eggs on. The eggs tend to hatch all at once, and the young caterpillars can eat entire plants overnight. Visual inspection by checking the undersides of leaves for the yellow eggs is a good step towards reducing outbreaks, while a physical barrier of netting (see Protecting vegetables, page 25) will stop the butterflies landing and laying on the crop. The caterpillars of pea moths also cause considerable damage, as the young hatch within the pea pod and cannot be seen until after harvest. Use fine netting to stop the tiny moths laying eggs or sow early cultivars (see Pea, page 102) because the eggs are laid during early summer and so can be avoided if the peas are harvested in late spring.

Root flies

These cause damage underground, and are often specific to the crop: for example, cabbage root flies attack brassica roots (see Cabbage, page 57); and carrot flies go for carrot roots (see Carrot, page 78) and sometimes parsnips (see page 97). In all cases, barrier protection is the most effective method of control to stop the adult fly laying its eggs in the root area of the crop, because it is the larvae that causes the damage. Place a cabbage collar over the root area of each brassica plant to stop access by the fly. Such collars are circular barriers, 10–15cm/4–6in wide, each with one slit to allow it to fit tightly against the stem of the plant while sitting flat on the soil. They can be purchased or easily made from material such as cardboard. The carrot fly cannot fly particularly high, so surround carrot plants with a 60cm/24in-tall micromesh barrier to prevent access. Because the carrot fly is attracted by the smell of crushed carrot leaves, you can also deter it by interplanting with an allium crop (see Alliums, page 13) or by being extremely careful when thinning the carrots. See also Protecting vegetables, page 25.

DISEASES

Diseases of vegetable crops are fungal, bacterial or viral. Fungal diseases tend to cause the most problems to crops, especially in the height of a humid summer.

Blight

A disease in the vegetable garden, which spreads quickly, is blight. It is a fungus-like disease that attacks tomatoes (see page 115) and potatoes (see page 121). It spreads during humid weather and shows itself as brown patches on the leaves with a white halo on the undersides. Blight causes stems and foliage to collapse and die; in tomatoes, the fruit is also affected. Potato tubers can be saved if the foliage is removed quickly enough. Resistant cultivars can be obtained to combat blight, and there are reporting systems which alert if blight is expected, so growers can harvest what they can of the crop. If blight does affect your crops, burn all infected material and rotate the growing area for the next year.

Clubroot
This is a parasitic disease of brassicas (see page 14) by *Plasmodiophora brassicae*, which live in the soil. It is related to slime mould and causes the roots to swell and it stunts growth. Treat clubroot by raising the soil pH to above 6.5 because the disease thrives in acidic soil.

Damping off
This fungal disease of seedlings is caused when seeds are sown too thickly, and air cannot flow easily. Damping off makes seedlings collapse and will quickly move through a greenhouse. To avoid this, make sure all pots and propagators are cleaned thoroughly and allow for good airflow, sowing seeds as thinly as possible.

Powdery mildew
Powdery mildew is a fungal disease that shows itself on the leaves of plants in the cucurbit family (Cucurbitaceae) during the humidity of summer. It appears as white patches. It starts on the oldest leaves and can transfer to the fruits, causing them to rot. The easiest way to manage an attack of powdery mildew is to remove the infected leaves and grow resistant varieties. Other vegetables that may suffer from powdery mildews include peas (page 102) and brassicas (see page 14). Again, the best treatment is removal of infected parts, but also keeping plants well watered will reduce attacks in the first place.

Viruses
Tomatoes (see page 115) can suffer from many viruses, which tend to distort the leaves or stop fruit setting. Once a virus is in a plant, the best course of action is to remove it, because the virus is often spread by vectors such as aphids (see page 132).

DISORDERS
These are environmental issues that affect plants and can, therefore, usually be corrected.

Calcium deficiency
A lack of calcium in tomatoes (see page 115), aubergines (see page 120) and peppers (see page 66) can show itself through blossom end rot, where dark patches appear on the undersides of fruits and then spread around the fruits, making them inedible. Not a true lack of calcium in the soil, it is actually caused by inconsistent watering, because calcium needs to be transported with a good water supply around the plant.

Nutrient deficiency
The most common disorder in vegetables is nutrient deficiency, with yellowing leaves often being a sign of too little nitrogen and with poor flowering and fruit set an indication that there is not enough potassium. Both of these can be corrected with a liquid feed (see Feeding, page 27). In the long term, ensure soils are cultivated and fertilized well, then none of these disorders should occur. Other nutrient deficiencies do appear, usually through the discoloration of the leaves, and it is worth researching these if the plant is showing physical signs of being ill.

What to do when

SPRING

Spring is the time of year when the vegetable garden truly begins to revive, the ground starts to warm and the daylight hours get longer, thereby providing the conditions to start sowing indoors and in the plot. In early spring it can still be cold and frosty so there is no rush, but a steady start to the season will give rewards later. Watch the ground not only for emerging weeds but also for the appearance of the perennial plants, which are welcome in the traditional 'hungry gap' in mid-spring, when there is little coming from the plot. Begin direct sowing in the vegetable garden once the soil feels warm to the touch 5cm/2in down, and is around 7°C/45°F. Use a thermometer to check this.

Growing
- In early spring, sow the early-summer crops (beetroot, turnips, pak choi, endive, watercress, spinach, spring onions) and those that need the cool of spring (calabrese, cabbages, kohl rabi, rocket). Seeds such as tomatoes, peppers, okra, oca, tomatillo, sweetcorn, celery, celeriac, peanuts and cucurbits are likely to need heat to protect them from frosts.
- In early spring, sow leeks in a seedbed; move to their final planting site in late spring.
- In mid-spring, sow leafy crops such as lettuce, chard, mizuna, buckler-leaf sorrel and spinach in modules.
- In mid-spring, plant chitted potatoes, onion sets and shallot sets.
- Sow French beans in pots indoors or *in situ* once the soil is consistently 12°C/54°F.
- Directly sow roots (carrots, swedes, lamb's lettuce, sweetcorn, parsley root, radishes, radish pods and parsnips), as well as mangetout into the ground.
- In late spring, sow carrots *in situ*, soya beans and runner beans in pots and sprouting broccoli and Brussels sprouts in modules.
- Slowly harden off plants that have been sown indoors with a view to planting out once there is little risk of frosts – these often occur in late spring.
- Plant perennial crops (American groundnuts, Jerusalem artichokes, seakale, asparagus, rhubarb) when the soil has warmed to around 7°C/45°F, and there is plenty of water to help them establish.

Maintaining
- Early spring is the last chance to cultivate soil, either by digging or mulching.
- Keep on top of weed removal at this time of year to avoid problems later in the season.
- Harvest spring rainwater to use throughout summer.

Harvesting
- In early spring, harvest overwintered crops such as

Chitting potatoes in a frost-free, light place can give an earlier crop.

cabbages, kale, chard, kohl rabi, mizuna, komatsuna, seakale, spinach, lamb's lettuce and sprouting broccoli, as well as the last of the parsnips and leeks, as they will attempt to put up flower heads and become woody.

- In mid-spring pick the perennial crops rhubarb, seakale and asparagus.
- If the season is warm, young leaves will be harvestable by late spring.
- In late spring, pick broad beans, early peas, carrots, radishes, spring onions, globe artichokes, radish pods, buckler-leaf sorrel and young beetroot.

SUMMER

The summer months are a bounty of heat, light and long days, meaning that you have more time in the vegetable garden. This is the time of year when the growing space can offer up the largest variety of crops and the vegetables begin to grow quickly, filling up the space provided for them. The produce comes thick and fast, and these fresh tastes are a relief after the winter months. Keep on top of the harvests to make the most of the plants, as some will stop producing if allowed to go to seed. The end of summer is also the time to be thinking about crops to overwinter.

Growing

- By early summer most cold weather should have passed so plant the last of the tender crops in the vegetable garden.
- In early summer, sow kale in a seed tray and soya beans in pots.
- Keep sowing salads both indoors and directly, for a constant supply.
- Sow other successional crops including beetroot, radishes, mangetout, radish pods, spinach, swedes and carrots.
- In midsummer, sow Florence fennel in modules or *in situ.*
- In mid- or late summer, begin sowing autumn and winter crops such as endive, chicory, lettuce, chard, miner's lettuce, komatsuna, lamb's lettuce, pak choi and cabbage. Start them in modules in order to allow summer crops to mature before these autumn vegetables need the space in the vegetable garden.
- In late summer, directly sow crops including swede, rocket, mizuna and turnip.

Maintaining

- Continue to remove weeds regularly, especially in early summer. Do not let them flower or set seed.
- Water crops when the weather is dry, always checking the water content below the surface, because a healthy soil may contain water even though the top centimetre or so is dry.
- Feed crops with liquid fertilizer where necessary especially fruiting crops, to continue healthy growth.
- Watch for pests and diseases, which may start to be more prevalent

Starting crops in modules is a good way to extend the growing season.

with the warmth and humidity of summer (see Troubleshooting, page 132).

Harvesting

- Continue harvesting salads and successional crops such as carrots, radishes, spring onions, radish pods, komatsuna, spinach, chard, cabbages and beetroot.
- In early summer, pick mangetout, the remaining peas and broad beans. Remember to save their seeds (see Seed saving, page 118).
- From early summer, harvest turnips, pak choi and potatoes.
- In mid- or late summer, pull up the garlic, shallots and onions, dry these thoroughly and store for the rest of the year.

- In mid- or late summer, harvest courgettes, cucumbers, French and runner beans, tomatoes, calabrese, cauliflowers, Florence fennel, cucamelon, tomatillo, agretti, aubergines, sweetcorn and peppers.
- In late summer, start picking okra and soya beans.

AUTUMN

The last of summer heat can still be felt in autumn, with the soil warm enough for last-minute crops to be sown directly. This is a time to store the tastes of summer by harvesting and preserving crops for winter use. The end of autumn can bring cold weather, so get to know when this generally occurs and harvest all tender plants by this point, to avoid disappointment.

Harvest leeks as required throughout autumn and winter, being careful not to damage the stems.

Growing
- Harden off and plant out chard.
- In early autumn, sow buckler-leaf sorrel, broad beans and peas for overwintering, starting them in pots and planting out once summer crops have been harvested.
- From mid-autumn, plant garlic *in situ*, to allow it to establish before winter.
- In early autumn, sow quick-maturing crops such as radish, turnip, lettuce and spinach directly; they should be harvestable before the first frosts.
- In early autumn, plant perennial plants (asparagus crowns, rhubarb crowns) while the soil is still warm.
- Dig up the roots of witloof chicory and prepare them for forcing (see Chicory, page 68).

Maintaining
- In late autumn, protect crops with horticultural fleece, to prolong harvesting.
- Continue regularly removing weeds, which will set seed quickly in the warm soil.
- Start mulching empty beds if using the no-dig method of cultivation.

Harvesting
- Continue harvesting okra, beetroot, chard, pak choi, endive, courgettes, carrots, rocket, lamb's lettuce, spinach, radishes, agretti, sweetcorn, Florence fennel, soya beans, cucamelon and watercress.
- Dig up celery, oca, celeriac, leeks, peanuts, swedes, chicory, miner's lettuce, Jerusalem artichokes, parsnips, parsley root and yacon.

Store root crops such as beetroot in a clamp so they are readily accessible for eating during the winter.

- Gather last harvests of, for example, tomatoes, peppers, carrots, aubergines, cucumbers and runner beans; they can be useful stored or preserved.
- Lift root crops such as potatoes and sweet potatoes, saving some for use next year if the plants have been disease-free.
- Harvest squash and pumpkins, and cure them for winter storage.
- Collect seeds for the following season from tomatoes, cucurbits, legumes and peppers (see Seed saving, page 118).
- Pull the last of the salad crops before the frosts arrive.

- Towards late autumn, crop brassicas including kale, calabrese, kohl rabi, mizuna, komatsuna, cabbages and cauliflowers.
- Harvest American groundnuts and store their tubers for the next season.

WINTER
There is still plenty to do in the vegetable garden over winter. Hardy crops will still give a harvest, and towards the end of winter seeds can be sown. Winter is a time of reflection and preparation, and these are key to a successful year in the vegetable garden.

Start crops that need a long growing season indoors, and give them artificial heat.

Growing

- Continue planting garlic *in situ* until mid-winter.
- In late winter, start sowing onions, shallots, spring onions, cauliflowers and calabrese. Long-season plants such as peppers, seakale, globe artichokes and aubergines can also be started now if heat can be provided.
- Provide supplementary lights for seedlings, if possible, because low light levels are the biggest issue at this time of year.
- In late winter, sow leeks, spring onions, agretti, peas, broad beans, mangetout, spinach and asparagus seeds under glass.
- In late winter, start sweet potatoes from slips (see page 88).

Maintaining

- Continue cultivating the soil, except when extremely wet because this causes compaction.
- Protect crops that are being overwintered with horticultural fleece if necessary.
- Clean and sharpen tools and pots.
- Wash the greenhouse to allow as much light to come through the windows and to reduce overwintering pests and diseases.
- Begin planning for next year and ordering seeds.

Harvesting

- In early winter, harvest turnips and winter radishes.
- Pick sprouting broccoli, parsnips, kale, cabbages, mizuna and Brussels sprouts. Growth will be slower, so only harvest what is needed and let plants rest in between harvests.
- Pick winter leaves under protection for a tasty salad. These often completely stop growing in mid-winter, so do not over-pick at this point.
- Continue cropping leeks, chard, swedes, endive, chicory, miner's lettuce, rocket, parsnips, spinach, Jerusalem artichokes and lamb's lettuce.

Index

Page numbers in *italics* indicate
an illustration or text in a box.
Page numbers in **bold** indicate
a main entry for a particular
vegetable. Note that all beans
are under 'beans' with a
subentry for particular types.

A
acid soils 13
agretti 113
air miles in vegetable transport 9
alkaline soils 13
allium leaf miner 26
alliums 13–14, *15*, **31–9**
American groundnut 40
annual crops 17
aphids *25*, 132
artichokes
  globe **77**
  Jerusalem **86**
arugula *see* rocket
asparagus 20, **44–5**
  creating a bed *46–7*
  for wildlife *72*
aubergines 14, **120**
autumn tasks **139–40**

B
Babbington leeks 14
basil, on windowsills *104*
beans
  Borlotti beans *100*
  broad beans *54*, **130**
    sowing 22
    supports *128–9*
  dwarf: raised beds *34*
    fertilizing 27
  French beans 16, *54*, *100*, *118*
  runner beans 17, **99**
    raised beds *34*
    supports 26
  soya beans **84–5**
  successional sowing 24
  for wildlife *72*
beetroot 17, **48**
  clamping *80*, *140*
  as decoration *54*
  heritage 9
  successional sowing 24
  on windowsills *104*
bell peppers *66*
bhindi *see* okra
biennial crops 17
bindweed, hedge 17
biodiesel from okra *30*
bird problems 132
bittercress, hairy 17
blackberries *72*
blight 134

bolting 33
brassicas 14, *15*
  hardiness 10
  protection 26
  rotation *21*
broccoli *53*, **61**
Brussels sprouts 14, **59**
  harvesting *124*
  successional sowing 24
buckler-leaf sorrel **112**
bulb fennel *see* Florence fennel
butterflies 26
butternut squash *75*
buying vegetables to grow 19–20

C
cabbage root flies 134
cabbage white butterfly *25*, 134
cabbages 14, 20, **57–8**
  Chinese *see* pak choi
  collars *132*, 134
  red *54*
  savoy *124*
  transplanting 23
  types *58*
calabrese **53**
calcium deficiency 135
calçots *37*
Calendula officinalis
  (pot marigolds) *25*, *72*
capsaicin *66*
capsicums *see* peppers
carrot flies 26, 134
carrots 16–17, **78–9**
  clamping *80–1*
  as decoration *54*
  harvesting *124*
  pest tolerance 20
  raised beds *34–5*
  seeds *118*
  sowing 22
  types *79*
Castroville Artichoke Festival
  77
catch cropping 24
caterpillars 134
Catherine de Medici, Queen *126*
cauliflowers 14, **56**
Cavolo Nero *52*
celeriac **42**
celery **41**
chard 9, **49**, *54*
chemicals, use of 9, *72*
chicory *11*, 15, **68**
chillies *25*, **66**
chitting *137*
choosing vegetables to grow
  19–20
clamping *80–1*
clay soil 12

cloches 19, 26
clubroot 135
cold frames 19, 23, 26
comfrey as fertilizer *27*, *72*
companion planting *25*, *72*, *107*
compost 27
compost heaps 18
coriander, on windowsills *104*
courgettes 9, 17, *54*, **74**
crop rotation *21*
cubio *see* oka
cucamelons 25, **92**
cucumbers 24, **71**
cucurbit powdery mildew 135
curly kale *52*
cut-and-come-again crops
  104–5
cynar *77*

D
damping off 135
decorative vegetables *54–5*
diseases **134–5**
disorders **135**

E
edamame *see* beans, soya
egg plant *see* aubergines
endive **67**
environmental issues 9

F
F1 cultivars 20
fertilizing the soil 18–19, 27
Florence fennel **83**
forcing *11*
Ford, Henry *84*
French sorrel *see* buckler-leaf
  sorrel
frost pockets *11*
frosting for sweetness *97*
fructooligosaccharides *114*
fruiting vegetables 14–15, *15*

G
garlic 13–14, **38–9**, *124*
German turnip *see* kohl rabi
globe artichokes **77**
glucosinolates *63*
green manure 18–19
greenhouses 25
groundnut, American 40

H
Hamburg parsley
  see parsley root
hardening off 23
hardiness 10
health benefits 10
hedges *72*

heritage vegetables 9
Hippocrates *93*
Hohensalzburg Castle *62*
horticultural fleece 19, 26
hoverflies *25*, *72*
Hubbard squash *75*
hygiene 19

I
Indian lettuce *see*
  miner's lettuce
intercropping 24

J
Jack o'lantern *76*
Japanese mustard greens *see*
  mizuna
Jersey walking stick 51
Jerusalem artichokes **86**

K
kale **51–2**
  curly *52*
  as decoration *54*
  harvesting *124*
  seeds *118*
  on windowsills *104*
Kew Gardens *54*, *122*
kohl rabi **60**
komatsuna **65**

L
lacewings *72*
Lacinto kale *52*
ladybirds *72*
lady's fingers *see* okra
lamb's lettuce *127*
leafy crops *see* salad crops
Leek Garden 31
leeks 13–14, **31**
  harvesting *124*, *139*
legumes *15*, 16, 27
  nitrogen fixation *99*
  protection 26
lettuce 9, 15, 16, *16*, 17, **90–1**
  as decoration *54*
  Indian *see* miner's lettuce
  miner's **69**
  sowing 22, 24
  types *91*
  on windowsills *104*
light needs 13
lignin *106*
Linnaeus, Carl *43*
loam soil 12

M
mad apple *see* aubergines
mangetout **106**
manure 27

marigolds
  French *see Tagetes*
  pot *see Calendula officinalis*
melons, in greenhouse 25
Mendel, Gregor *102*
Mexican sour gherkin *see*
  cucamelons
microclimates 10–11
microgreens *104–5*
micromesh 26
miner's lettuce **69**
mizuna **64**
modules 22–3, *138*
molleboon 130
Monroe, Marilyn *77*
mouse melon *see* cucamelons
mulching 18, *18*, 27
mustards, on windowsills
  104

N
nasturtium *see*
  Tropaeolum majus
netting 26, *103*
nettles 27
New Zealand yam *see* oka
nitrogen content 27
nitrogen deficiency 135
nitrogen fixation *99*
no-dig cultivation 18, *72*
nutrient deficiency 135

O
oca 10, **96**
okra 30
onions 13–14, **32–3**
  harvesting *124*
  sets vs seeds *33*
  watering 26–7
opium, lettuce *91*
organic gardening 9, 20
organic matter for soils 12

P
pak choi 10, **63**
parsley on windowsills *104*
parsley root **98**
parsnips 16–17, **97**
  harvesting *124*
  raised beds *35*
  seeds *118*
  successional sowing 24
pea moths 134
pea shoots *103*, *104*
peanuts **43**
peas 16, **102–3**
  as decoration *54*
  mangetout **106**
  successional sowing 24
  sugar snap **106**

supports 26
  for wildlife *72*
peppers 9, 14, **66**
  as decoration *54*
  in greenhouse 25, 17
  sowing 22
  sweet *66*
  transplanting 22–3, 23
perennial crops 17
Peruvian ground apple
  see yacon
pests **132–4**
Phacelia tanacetifolia 18–19
phosphorus 27
physalis *see* tomatillo
pigeons 26, *103*
pinching out 116
planning vegetable plot 13
planting out 23–4
plug plants 20
pollination *115*
polytunnels 25
potassium 27
potassium deficiency 135
potato bean *see* American
  groundnut
potatoes 17, **121–3**
  chitting *137*
  clamping *80*
  fertilizing 27
  harvesting *124*
  sweet *see* sweet potatoes
  types *123*
powdery mildew 135
preparation of plot 17–18
pricking out 22
Prometheus *83*
propagation
  rooting watercress *94–5*
  sweet potato slips *88–9*
propagator 19, 22
protecting vegetables 25–6
pumpkins 14, **76**
purslane, winter *see* miner's
  lettuce

R
radicchio *68*
radish pods **108**
radishes 9, 24, *54*, *107*
raised beds **34–5**
Rapunzel *127*
rhubarb **109**
  buying 20
  forced *11*, *109*, *110–11*
Rhubarb Triangle *109*
rocket 14, 16, **82**, *104*
root flies 134
root vegetables *15*, 16–17
  clamping *80–1*

raised beds *34*
  rotation *21*
rooting watercress *94–5*
roses *72*
rutabaga *see* swede

S
salad crops 14–15, *15*, *104–5*
salad onions *see* spring onions
salad rocket *see* rocket
sandita *see* cucamelons
sandy soil 12
scallions *see* spring onions
scapes *39*
Scoville scale *66*
seakale *11*, *70*, *110*
seedlings 22, 135
seeds
  saving 20, *118–19*
  sowing 20–2
senposai **65**
shallots **36**
shelter 11
silty soil 12
Sinapsis alba 18–19
siting 10–11, 13
sloes *72*
slugs 27, *103*
soil pH 12, 13
soil-testing kit *12*
sorrel
  buckler-leaf *112*
  types *112*
  on windowsills *104*
sowing seeds 20–2
soya beans *see under* beans
spinach 15, **126**
spinach mustard,
  on windowsills *104*
spring beauty *see* miner's lettuce
spring onions **37**
spring tasks **136**
sprouts *see* Brussels sprouts
squashes 14
  fertilizing 27
  successional sowing 24
  summer **74**
  watering 27
  winter *74*, **75**
strawberries 27
  successional sowing 24
sugar beet *48*
sugar snap peas **106**
sugarloaf chicory *68*
summer tasks **137–8**
suppengrun *98*
supports 24, 26, 116, *128–9*
swedes *50*, *80*, *124*
sweet potatoes **87**, *88–9*
sweetcorn 24,**131**

T
Tagetes (French marigolds) *25*
thermometer 19
toad beetroot 9
tomatillo **101**
tomatoes 14, **115–17**
  as decoration *54*
  diseases 135
  in greenhouse 25
  hardiness 10
  seeds 20, 22, 116, *118*
  supports 116
  transplanting 23
  types *117*
  watering 116
tools 19
transplanting 22–3
Tropaeolum majus (nasturtium)
  25, *72*
Turkish rocket *82*
turnips 14, **62**
  clamping *80*
  German *see* kohl rabi
  usefulness or not 19
Tuscan kale *52*
Tusky *109*

U
uqa *see* oka

V
vermiculite 22
viruses 135

W
water in garden *72*
watercress **93**, *94–5*
watering 26–7
weeds 17–19
Welsh onions 14
wildlife friendly vegetable
  garden *72–3*
winter purslane *see* miner's
  lettuce
winter tasks **140–1**
Witloof/Belgian chicory *68*
woodchip 27

Y
yacon **114**
yams, New Zealand *see* oka

First published in 2020 by Frances Lincoln, an imprint of The Quarto Group.
The Old Brewery, 6 Blundell Street
London, N7 9BH,
United Kingdom
T (0)20 7700 6700 F (0)20 7700 8066
www.QuartoKnows.com

A catalogue record for this book is available from the British Library.

ISBN 978-0-7112-4278-4

10 9 8 7 6

Typeset in Stempel Garamond and Univers
Design by Arianna Osti

Printed in China

MIX
Paper from responsible sources
FSC
www.fsc.org   FSC® C016973

Acknowledgments

I would like to say a huge thank you to all those who have supported me in writing this book: to Martin, who has been there every step of the way and is now a master in dealing with gluts of courgettes and green tomatoes; to Liz, Laura, Alix, Lou, Stiggles, Mark and Pin, you have all provided me with coffee and beers and listened to me babble about vegetables with a large amount of patience and smiles, for which I am ever grateful; and to Mum, Val and Dad, for encouraging my love of growing from an early age.

Thank you to Joe Archer and Martin O'Halloran, for bringing me to Kew and continuing to support my work in the Kitchen Garden. Kew Publishing have been fantastic and a joy to work with, so thank you to Gina Fullerlove and her team, who make these projects possible. A big thanks also goes to Joanna Chisholm and Helen Griffin, for guiding me through the process of producing a book.

Photographic acknowledgements

a=above; b=below; m=middle; l=left; r=right

© Alamy 11 FLPA, 133 Matthew Taylor, 139 Alison Thompson

© Hélèna Dove 15bl, 47, 55, 73mr, 81, 86, 89, 95, 105, 111, 112, 119, 125ml, 125b, 129, 141

© GAP Photos 18 Gary Smith, 73b Gary Smith, 85 Leigh Clapp, 140

© Shutterstock 6–7 EsHanPhot, 8 Hquality, 12 Sarah2, 15al MargoLLL, 15am Doikanoy, 15ar Peter Turner Photography, 15bm Ctatiana, 15br Annaev, 16 Alexander Raths, 23 TanaCh, 24 Katarzyna Mazurowska, 25 Swellphotography, 27 zlikovec, 28–9 nnattalli, 30 Videowokart, 31 Graham Corney, 33 yuris, 35al Del Doy, 35ar HildaWeges Photography, 35ml Del Boy, 35mr Vintagepix, 35b lunamarina, 36 RusticFOTO, 37 jgolby, 39a alicja neumiler, 39b yuris, 40 Danny Hummel, 41 Zigzag Mountain Art, 42l A la Musubi, 45 Africa Studio, 50 Michaelpuche, 52ml Vezzani Photography, 52br Peter Turner Photography, 53 Morlaya, 58 Peter Turner Photography, 60 giedre vaitekune, 63 annarepp, 64l Ryoko Fujiwara, 64r lamnee, 65l kariphoto, 65r lamnee, 68 Peter Turner Photography, 69 avoferten, 70 PosiNote, 71 Africa Studio, 73al Peter Turner Photography, 73ar Lertwit Sasipreyajun, 73ml Graham Corney, 79 Graham Corney, 82 vaivirga, 83 NataLima, 84 nnattalli, 90 Mirage_studio, 91 Suwicha, 92l Olgalele, 92r ArtCookStudio, 93 doolmsch, 96 CreativeMedia.org.uk, 97 Peter Polak, 98 Manfred Ruckszio, 101 Chatsushutter, 102 igorstevanovic, 103 FlorinRO, 107 Henrique Lima BR, 108 Niwat Sripoomsawatt, 109 MarinaKarkizova, 113 P T Pictures, 114l Alice Heart, 114r lamnee, 117 Joanna Tkaczuk, 123 Peter Turner Photography, 125al Graham Corney, 125ar Deyan Georgiev, 125mr Lena Kudim, 126 Peter Turner Photography, 127 corners74, 137 Swellphotography, 138 veou